# INVESTIGATING WONDERS

## Age of Mystery Book II

Dr. Harry Assad Salem III

INVESTIGATING WONDERS Age of Mystery
Book II
ISBN 1-890370-38-X

Second Printing
Copyright © 2017 by Salem Family Ministries

Salem Family Ministries
PO Box 1595
Cathedral City, CA 92235
www.salemfamilyministries.org

Disclaimer: The views expressed in this book contain my personal opinions, theories, and experiences throughout my life and time spent in God's word and private research. I express them as my opinion and views only, and share them with you from my lifelong experience and research. I am only communicating what has been revealed to me, and what I have personally studied and researched.

# DEDICATION

THIS BOOK IS DEDICATED TO MY NEPHEW ROMAN
HARRY SALEM JR. WHOSE SLEEP OVERS HELPED ME
TO FOCUS AND GET THE WORK DONE.

# CONTENTS

# ACKNOWLEDGMENTS

To Mai Van whose art pieces always motivated me when I sought inspiration.

# ABBREVIATIONS

AD- After Domini


BC- Before Christ


ESV- English Standard Version


ISIS- Islamic State of Iraq and Syria


KJV- King James Version


NIV- New International Version


UNESCO- United Nations Educational Scientific and Cultural Organization

# GLOSSARY

**ABORIGINAL**- someone or something that has existed or inhabited a place from early times before later inhabitants.

**ANIMISM**- a religious or cult practice of believing living and nonliving things has their own spirit or spiritual qualities.

**ANTRHOPORMORPHISM**- a religious or cult practice of attributing human traits with animals, nature, emotions, and other things.

**ASSIANISM- a** monistic religion believing with all natures being the same.

**TSEBAAH**- Hebrew word for persons, soldiers, or host.

**BAMAH**- Hebrew word for high place. A sanctuary or religious site used by Israelites and non-Israelites.

**BENE ELOHIM**- sons of God (angels). Is a phrase used in the Hebrew Bible and Apocrypha. The phrase is also used in Kabbalah where Bene Elohim is part of different Jewish angelic hierarchies.

**BUDDHISM**- belief system from India that says all life is suffering and is caused by desire.

**ECOLOGY**- the biology branch dealing with the relationship of organisms and their physical surroundings.

**GIANT**- a very tall person. A mythical human of very great size.

**GILGAL**- Hebrew word for cult site. A circular type enclosure used for religious reasons. A location in the book of Joshua where ancient Israel encamped and performed circumcision.

**HYBRID**- an offspring resulting from crossbreeding.

**HINDUISM**- A Vedic religion from India.

**ISLAM**- a monotheistic religion of worship to one god referred to as Allah.

**MONOTHEISM**- belief in a single god.

**NATUFIANS**- refers to the Epipaleolithic culture from 12,500 BC to 9,500 BC. Famous for agriculture, and cult practices such as plastered skulls and zoomorphic carvings.

**NAGAS**- serpent deities in Indian mythology.

**NEPHILIM**- were the offspring of the sons of God and the daughters of men before the deluge or flood of Noah.

**PANTHEISM**- belief that the universe is a manifestation of God. Belief that tolerates all gods.

**POLEMICAL**- multiple arguments used to support specific positions or a specific position.

**POLYTHEISM**- belief in multiple gods.

**PROGENITOR**- something or someone from which other things or other people originate or begin.

**SCYTHIANS**- were a large group of Iranian Eurasian nomads who were mentioned by the literate peoples surrounding them as inhabiting large areas in the central Eurasian steppes from about the 9$^{th}$ century BC until about the 1$^{st}$ century BC.

**SEMITE**- relates to languages of Hebrew, Arabic, Aramaic, and other ancient or dead languages such as Akkadian. Refers to the Jewish people in modern and ancient times as well as other minor groups that spoke Semitic language such as Amorites.

**SERAPHIM**- is a type of celestial or heavenly being in Christianity and Judaism. Highest rank of angel in the Christian angelic hierarchy and in the fifth rank of ten in the Jewish angelic hierarchy.

**SHAMANISM**- a religious or cult practice of having an alternate state of mind to connect to the spirit world. One who practices shamanism is considered a shaman.

**SHINTOISM**- also called Shinto. A Japanese religious belief that incorporates ancestor worship and belief in nature spirits.

**SPELEOTHEM**- secondary mineral deposits found in caves. Used for tools and other materials by early humans.

**TARTARUS**- is the deep abyss that is used as a dungeon of torment and suffering for the wicked and as a prison for the Titans in Greek Mythology.

**TERAPHIM**- Hebrew word for small cult objects usually made in humanlike shapes or plastered human skulls. Used for divination as oracles or as representations of deities by Semitic peoples. Massive group of plastered skulls believed to be teraphim were discovered at the Biblical city of Jericho.

**TROGLODYTE**- one who dwells or lives in a cave. A cave man.

**UBAIDIANS**- refers to the Ubaid culture of 6500 BC to 3800 BC. Derived from Tell al-'Ubaid where the earliest excavation of Ubaid period material occurred. Famous for agricultural breakthroughs, early architecture, hunting, and cult practices.

**ZORASTRIANISM**- A religion that is considered one of the oldest monotheistic religions in the world. Founded by the prophet Zoraster around 3500 years ago in ancient Iran.

**ZOOMORPHISM**- a religious or cult practice that attributes animals with humans or other things. Egyptian gods are examples of zoomorphism.

# FORWARD

It is important to constantly grow in learning and understanding. Wisdom and knowledge never end, but always begin anew again and again. Accepting that fact will expand ones thinking to levels of intelligence that one might not have ever thought possible. With the study of Tsz-Nephilimus Sapiens comes the opportunity to continue that growth.

History and mythology often overlap due to the events of real people being taken out of context as they turned into figures of legend, romanticized fantasy, or exaggerated additions to their feats. Proof is based in first breaking down myth to meet fact. When fact is discovered, then truth can follow. This is the gap between history and myth, science and philosophy, truth and exaggeration.

Proverbs 4:25 ESV reads, *"Let your eyes look directly forward, and your gaze be straight before you."* When we keep our eyes up and focused, the world appears right before us. It is larger than what is seen when we look at the ground where only our feet and the dirt exist. Knowledge acts very much like looking up from the ground. When we open a book and turn the page to the next one and the next, then we learn more rather than just simply staying stuck on page one with the same information before us. We shape our future by embracing our past, and we expand upon discovery by seeing and adding to what others have discovered and taught. To expand on an existing theory or replace it is the next step in becoming more like God in truth and wisdom.

This book will be covered in two sections. The first section will cover scientific, mythological, and anthropological research. The second section will deal with historical and archaeological research. Both sections work together to bring the knowledge and research in this book into harmony to better help readers learn and understand all the information that is in the following pages.

The information in this book is based off of my own research and theories as a scholar, historian, and archaeologist. While much of the information may have never been thought of by those who read it, every piece of information has been carefully researched and explained in detail to give the reader explicit and exact knowledge to help them know exactly what is being taught to them from scripture, science, and history to help connect the dots of all that is contained in the following chapters.

# SECTION I

# SCIENCE, MYTHOLOGY, & ANTHROPOLOGY

# CHAPTER 1: THE ODYSSEY OF LIFE

The age of the earth is estimated to be about 4.543 billion years old. The universe is estimated to be about 14 billion years old. There is a vastness to the history of both the universe and the earth that mankind has barely pulled from the dust to the surface to see what is underneath.

Euclidian geometry has its beginnings in triangles. The equilateral triangle has all sides of the same length, thus making them all equal to each other. This means that an equilateral triangle with vertices of ABC all line up equally to each other. Albert Einstein's theory of relativity implicates that the universe is not Euclidean. However, if we look at the intricate span of life and materials within the realm of what we perceive as the universe, then we can see an equality theory of life interacting on an equal level as one thing works with another thing to better survive and thrive.

From the beginnings of creation came the need for all things to work together in creation and destruction. When something is destroyed, something else takes its place. When something is created, it takes the place of something else. Something created can also live in harmony with other things, or become chaotic and not coexist. Destruction and creation can work together at the same time in terms of equal functioning. Death and life are equal to each other. What makes them different is how death and life affect different lives. The earth has seen multiple extinction and creation events long before even the first dinosaur stepped on land. The earliest living thing in existence was vegetation. Genesis 1:11 KJV says, *"And God said, Let the earth bring forth grass, the herb yielding seed, and the fruit tree yielding fruit after his kind, whose seed is in itself, upon the earth: and it was so."* Earth began with plants and similar life forms to plants.

From earths Precambrian era (4.6 billion years ago) came the earliest of microscopic life forms. Algae and single-celled bacteria were the first life forms to come into existence. Fossil evidence from Paleo-botany has allowed us to see the remains of all kinds of plant life. Algae from the sea became the soil for which all plants such as grass and trees grow. This would allow oxygen to come into existence. The earth possibly started with a nitrogen based atmosphere. With the emergence of algae known as Blue-green algae came the nitrogen trapping mechanisms called Liverworts that grew on the algae that fed the soil that formed from the algae. Over the next several million years would come a conversion of nitrogen to oxygen that would make for the creation and formation of more plant and complex life forms. Next would come the creatures of the seas and oceans, and the birds of the air.

The creatures of the sea and fowls of the air would come during what is called the Cambrian period about 550 million years ago. These animals appearing on the planet before land creatures matches up perfectly with Genesis 1:20-21 KJV, "*And God said, Let the waters bring forth abundantly the moving creature that hath life, and fowl that may fly above the earth in the open firmament of heaven. And God created great whales, and every living creature that moveth, which the waters brought forth abundantly, after their kind, and every winged fowl after his kind: and God saw that it was good.*"

According to history, sea creatures came first, and then came powerful winged fowl of the air. Fowl includes not only birds but also any winged creature that occupied the skies. Average people consider many of the earliest species of flying creature's dinosaurs. The word fowl is usually used to describe birds, however the term applies also to ancient winged creatures prior and up to the Cretaceous period that are classified as the ancestors of birds, but are not dinosaurs. After this would come the creatures that would walk on dry land.

The era of land creatures began with the Devonian Era about 408 MYA (million years ago). This was when dinosaurs and other land creatures began to spread over the face of the earth. From dinosaurs would come the use of stronger fertilization for better soil and more plant life that would make the earth more oxygen rich for mammals and the first humans. Dinosaurs were divided into two percentage groups. Herbivores making up about 65% of the dinosaur population, and 35% being carnivores. With so many plant eaters on the planet would come more potent fertilizer to produce richer soil for plants to grow. Mega flora (large vegetation) such as large trees, flowers, grass, and algae would grow and make more oxygen for the environment. When the dinosaurs went extinct, man became the apex (top of a pyramid) animal. With the extinction of the dinosaurs came the creation of fossil fuels. Fossil fuels allowed mankind to enter into the machine age with the introduction of cars, planes, ships, and the industrial revolution. The dinosaurs contributed to the creation of the earth that mankind would one day emerge. With their extinction would come the next steps for mankind to take into the technological age.

Mankind would spawn several species that would come into existence during the Cenozoic era. The earth was far different in the early days of the Cenozoic era where there was a much different earth than what we have presently. The oceans of the world were far drier than they were today. Antarctica was possibly a green and lush area instead of the frozen land of glaciers it is now.

Land was more available as the oceans and sea levels were much lower. Earth had a much more breathable and fresh oxygen atmosphere that allowed for better life expectancy, richer and wholesome food, and possibly more docile animals. Let me be clear to say that predators existed on the earth and killed to survive. However, it is very likely that many animals that we see today and their ancestors could at least be more pleasant to be around. Perhaps some of the more aggressive species could even be tamed or trained to live among humans.

I believe that mankind had two distinct original species of Homo Sapiens and Tsz-Nephilimus Sapiens. From those two species breeding and interbreeding would come the next generations and diverse species of mankind. Those species would live for a time, then quickly go the way of the dinosaur and become extinct. The only exception between dinosaurs and mankind is the possibility that the genetics of a few of the extinct human species got passed on through genetic drift into modern humans.

It has been confirmed that Neanderthals and Homo Sapiens did interbreed and produce offspring. It is likely that the DNA of many Neanderthal species survived into later generations of Homo sapiens. Around the globe, many people do produce traits that make them appear similar to Neanderthals. The same can be said of certain people looking like Homo Erectus and Homo Habilis. Homo Habilis is one of the earliest human fossils ever discovered. Dated to have lived between 2.3 and 1.4 MYA, the remains of Homo Habilis have been found in Africa in such places as Tanzania and Kenya. While having some more similarities to some early ape fossils, Homo Habilis had a larger brain, more flexible hands, straight fingers with more sensitivity, and used hand tools that were created from stone. Chimpanzees use tools such as rocks and twigs that are scavenged from various areas, but Homo Habilis made their own tools. The mention of the traits of Homo Habilis is to show that while both apes and man occupy the primate order, mankind is superior to ape by way of major differences in physical characteristics, brain size, and creativity.

The species of Homo Habilis is smaller than average humans. A recent discovery of a smaller species of human called Homo Naledi was discovered in 2015. Unearthed in South Africa, Homo Naledi was a small species of human that had a unique endocranial (inside of the human cranium) volume that was very small. These humans were about five feet tall in the males, with smaller sizes in the females. What makes Homo Naledi interesting of note is that the physical and physiological characteristics have led scientists to conclude that the species most likely is a hybrid species.

This human species most likely was born and thrived in several parts of Africa. No dating of how old Homo Naledi has been conducted yet as the fossils are very fragile and could be damaged or partially destroyed if radio carbon dating dated the fossils passed 50,000 years. The reason for this is due to the fact that in order to discover if a fossil is older than 50,000 years would then destroy the samples used in order to get a reasonable dating of the age of the fossil. However, many geologists believe that the caves in South Africa that Homo Naledi was discovered in are only 3 million years old.

Homo Naledi is an interesting human specimen. The entirety of the specimens that have been discovered share the same height and size among most of the other discovered remains and specimens.

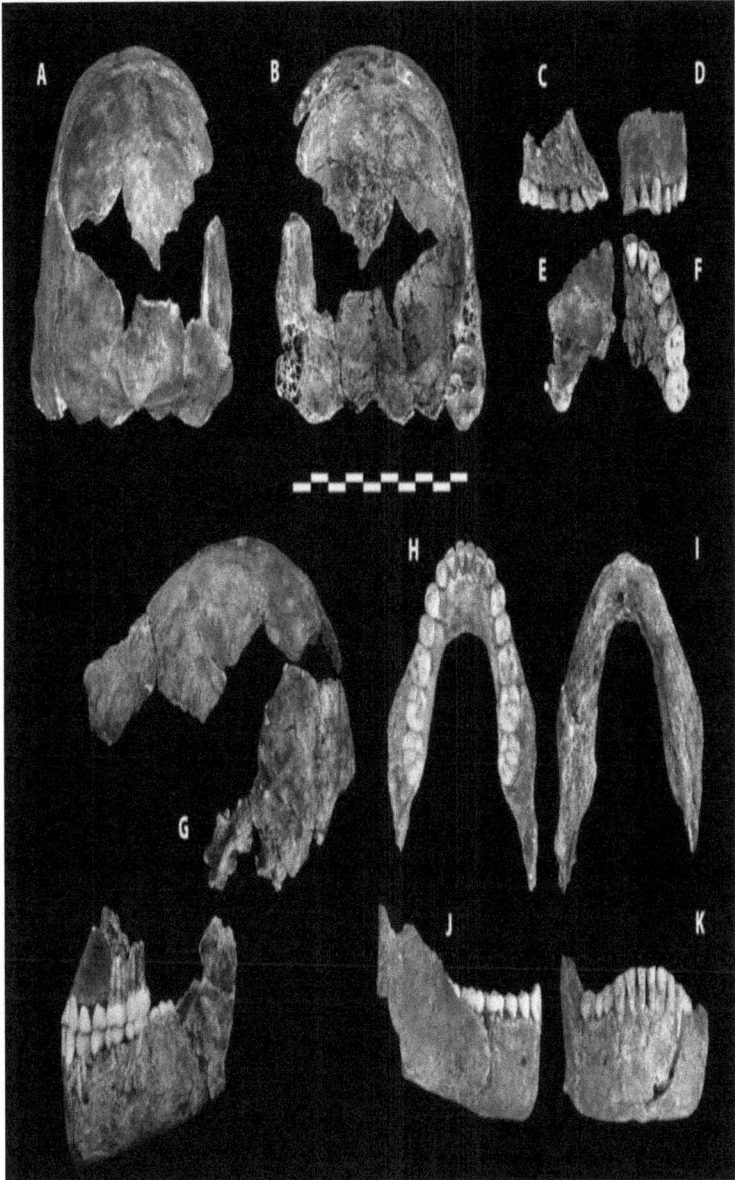

*Homo Naledi Remains Courtesy of The Lee Roger Berger Research Team*

Other specimens of what could be considered Human remains are discovered in the country of Indonesia. Specimens of ancient human species called Meganthropus (Meganthropus Palaeojavanicus) and Homo Floresiensis were discovered in Indonesia.

Meganthropus was estimated to be 9 to 10 feet tall in height. With Meganthropus, another species known as Homo Floresiensis was discovered in Indonesia. Homo Floresiensis is called the hobbit (referenced from author J.R.R. Tolkien's creatures in his books *The Hobbit and The Lord of The Rings*) due to its short height of about 3.5 feet tall. We have two unique human specimens to work with in order to identify some theories of the origins of humanity. If Meganthropus is older than Homo Floresiensis, then the possibility of a size evolution took place in Indonesia over time to allow future sizes to develop and adapt.

Tsz-Nephilimus Sapiens could have produced the genetic strain that would bring both large size to Meganthropus, and over time give rise to smaller generations of descendants due to possible genetic anomalies in the gene pool such as a possible state of dwarfism that took dominion as dwarfism has over 200 conditional causes. This is possibly due to the fact that the descendants of Tsz-Nephilimus Sapiens may have had created certain kinds of genetic disorders and diseases that would evolve over time with the changes in the ecologies and environments of the earth.

Romans 8:20-21 KJV says, *"For the creature was made subject to vanity, not willingly, but by reason of him who hath subjected the same in hope, because the creature itself also shall be delivered from the bondage of corruption into the glorious liberty of the children of God."*

Change is not often a willing process, but a process that takes place without consent. This is the way of life as many things are not within our control. Extinct species often face this truth as they have nowhere else to go but death. In the next chapter we will explore the idea of how the original human hybrids gave rise to genetic disorders that would eventually lead other human species into extinction.

# CHAPTER 2: ORIGIN, EXTINCTION, & CONTINUATION

Viruses and diseases have always plagued the world. The animal kingdom, mankind, and plant life all have their viruses and diseases that interact individually and with each other. Depending on the circumstances, viruses and diseases can be created from multiple sources. It is likely that early humans birthed all sorts of viral infections and diseases that would affect every other species of mankind.

The development of viruses and disease begins with RNA or ribonucleic acid. RNA composes the main genetic information of viruses. These are known as RNA viruses. RNA can become DNA through mutation. Mutation of RNA is done through exposure to ultraviolet lights or UV rays, gamma rays or radiation, certain chemical combinations, or by simple spontaneity. Just as animal species can evolve through mutation of RNA and DNA, so too can viruses and diseases.

The earliest living life forms on planet earth were plants. Algae and bacteria made up the earliest vegetation that used photosynthesis to survive by the absorption of sunlight that turned into plant food. Accordingly, plants would also be the earliest creatures to create diseases and viruses as they also affect plants just like animals and humans. Romans 5:12 KJV says, "*Wherefore, as by one man sin entered into the world, and death by sin; and so death passed upon all men, for that all have sinned.*"

The Greek word *anthropoi* is used to describe both men and women in reference to the whole of humanity. Everything in life is interconnected. From one thing can spring another. Like the offspring of two parents, viruses and diseases can occur from an original host. If we are to consider the size variations in multiple human species being the result of a genetic factor created from the combination of mutation with environment and possible genetic abnormality from the result of such things as inherited disease or viral infections that remained in the blood of a host parent that was passed on to a child, then we can see a unique equation of life with the final answer being adaption or extinction as a result of the effects that were inherited from a parent carrier of the genetics that would eventually make or break a species as a whole.

Let us take a look at the Zika virus for an example of a carry over genetic factor from a host parent to offspring. Discovered in 1947 in the Zika Forest of Uganda, the virus was first found in a monkey species that was being administered the virus by scientists of the Rockefeller Foundations Yellow Fever Research Institute. Labeled Rhesus 766 (a monkey from Asia instead of the local African breeds was used to test resistance in foreign specimens), the Zika virus was inserted into the monkey via mosquito bites in the hopes of identifying if the virus was indeed carried by the local bloodsuckers. The test proved the mosquitoes did carry the virus, that foreign primates such as Rhesus 766 could become infected and develop symptoms, and that the local monkeys possibly carried the virus but developed an immunity to it as the Zika virus may have existed for thousands of years and the local monkey population adapted to the virus with an immunity developed from one generation to the next until the virus was no longer a threat.

Zika is what is known as a Flavivirus. Flavivirus uses the Latin name *Flavi*, which means yellow. This is due to the virus being named for its most famous member called Yellow Fever. The Zika virus is for all accounts a non-death related virus with only a very minor rate of death due to certain victims having other health issues. However, the virus is life-threatening for yet to be born babies. The virus can penetrate the placenta of a pregnant woman. This then makes the still developing fetus or partially formed child experience birth issues such as Microcephaly. Microcephaly is a condition of the shrinking of the head of a child causing multiple problems such as brain damage, difficulty breathing, visual problems, certain cases of temporary paralysis, and death depending on the over all effects on the newborn.

The Zika virus has yet to be treated with modern medical treatments. There is no cure for it. It is estimated that with the current status of development of a treatable vaccine, the actual amount of time it would take to make a cure for the Zika virus

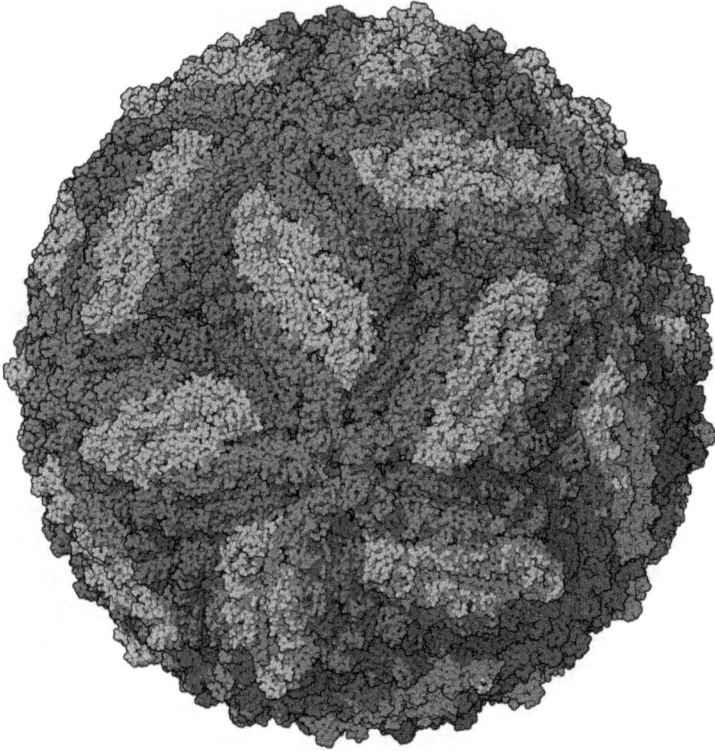

*Zika Virus Envelope Model Courtesy of Manuel Almagro Rivas*

would be two years with an extra 12 before the treatment would receive FDA approval for administering to actual human beings. For all accounts and reasons, by the time a treatment is approved, the Zika virus could mutate into a stronger form, a deadlier strain, more deadly or complicated symptoms could develop for humans, or mankind could simply adapt to the virus like the monkeys in Uganda did that appeared to be immune to the virus.

In the book and movie *Jurassic Park* by Michael Crichton, the DNA that was used to create the dinosaurs of the park were extracted from the remains of ancient mosquitoes. While a work of fiction, there is proof that DNA samples from extinct species such as dinosaurs could be in existence even after millions of years of decomposition in the grounds of the earth. The existence of such old DNA all depends on the preservation and condition of the bones that the dinosaurs and other animals were in during their long sleep in the earth.

In *Jurassic Park,* the extinct mosquitoes that were used for the harvesting of the dinosaur DNA were preserved in amber that had hardened over time becoming a perfectly preserved fossil. The practice in paleontology and entomology of finding extinct or ancient insects is actually accomplished by finding specimens in fossilized amber (tree sap). From the realization that such specimens can be found, then the next step is to study the ancient species or ancestors of the current mosquito populations that carries the Zika Virus.

Several species of mosquito that carry the Zika Virus belongs to the Aedes genus or family. The main mosquito species that carry the virus is Aedes Egyptica or the Yellow Fever Mosquito. Other species are the Aedes Africanus, Aedes Apicoargenteus, Aedes Luteocephalus, Aedes Albopictus, Aedes Vittatus, Aedes Furcifer, Aeded Hensilli, and Aedes Polynesiensis. Both Aedes Hensilli and Aedes Polynesiensis are South Pacific and French Polynesian mosquitos. These species of mosquito are tropical and subtropical mosquitoes that are found on all continents except Antarctica. These mosquitoes are spread both by natural means and human activity. The word Aedes is a Greek word meaning unpleasant or odious. Aside from Zika, these insects can carry all sorts of diseases such as Dengue Fever and Yellow Fever. They can be identified by the black and white markings on their bodies and legs. They are able to bite individuals during the daytime unlike other mosquito species that tend to be active after dusk. The genus contains over 700 species aside from the already mentioned members.

Jeremiah 26:1 KJV states, *"And I will smite the inhabitants of this city, both man and beast: they shall die of a great pestilence."* Mosquitoes are considered a pestilence (more on pestilence will be covered). Mosquitoes are an intrusive and invasive species that can affect whole populations of people ranging from a small community to an entire nation. The Zika virus is the great pestilence that smites a cities inhabitants.

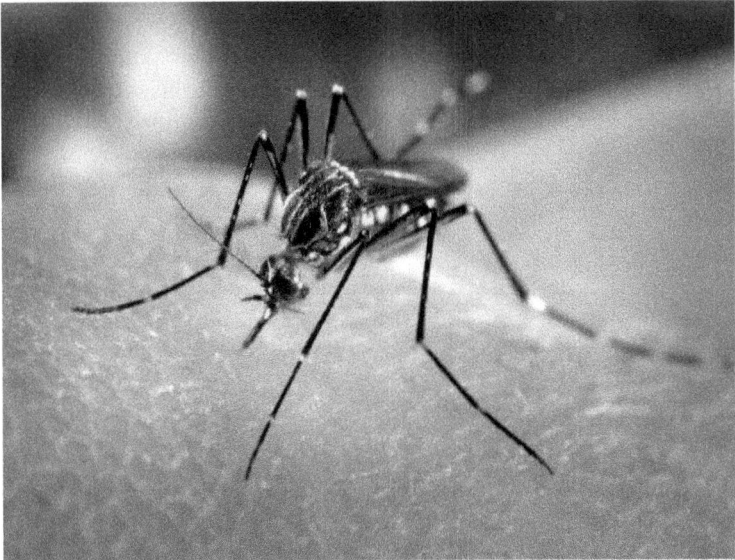

*Aedes Aegypti or Yellow Fever Mosquito Courtesy of James Gathany*

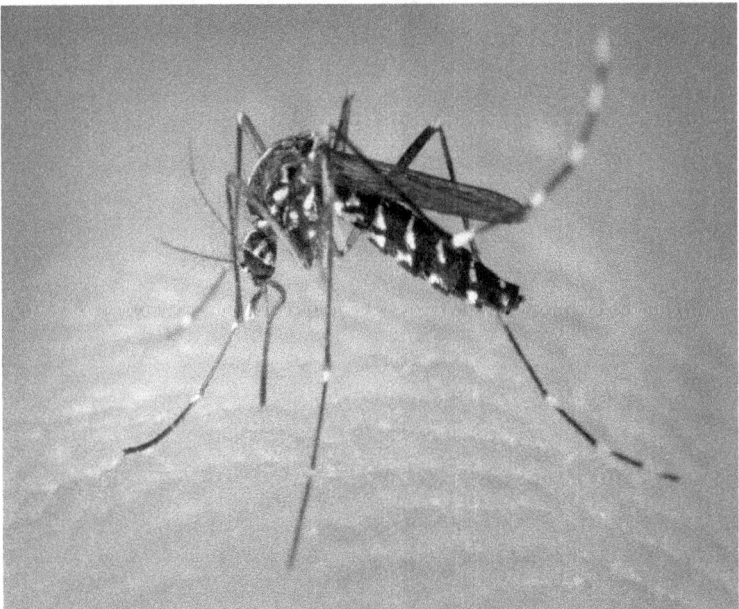

* *Aedes albopictus or Tiger Mosquito Courtesy of James Gathany*

What can be gathered from the study of the Zika virus is the possibility that the virus itself, or an older ground zero (the original virus) variation was present in the days when mankind was made up of multiple species. One condition that is produced by the Zika virus, Microcephaly, has characteristics that are seen in a few of the older human species. Microcephaly is a medical condition that makes the brain not develop properly, and thus produces a smaller sized cranium. This is a result of several possible factors such as chromosome abnormalities. The homozygous mutation of the microcephalin (a gene that is expressed during the fetal brain development process) gene, which is the cause of microcephaly, is where the disorder derives its name. While it is a disorder that has expectations of shorter life expectancy and lack lower brain functions, there is also a small rate of normal growth and lacking of normal intelligence development. Homo Floresiensis and Homo Naledi display very small craniums with small brain sizes.

Matthew 15:13 KJV, *"But he answered and said, 'Every plant, which my heavenly Father hath not planted, shall be rooted up.'"* Out of all the human species that have survived into the modern age, Homo Sapiens reign supreme. When considering genetic drift, many types of human species possibly pass on many kinds of genetic abnormalities to their offspring similar to how a mother or father can pass on a strain of the Zika virus to their offspring. As time passes and the environment changes, new generations come forward, and new strains of viruses and diseases arise due to mutations and other factors.

Next would come a possible attack on a human's health and well-being. If an immune system is not strong enough, then it is very likely that the human species would slowly start to go extinct. With genetic drift, if there is not enough of an allele source to continue to survive, a species will ultimately die off. In other abnormal mutations such as polydactyly and dwarfism, the results of such disorders are due to certain things such as fake sex chromosomes forming in place of insufficient new genetic material to use for a perfectly healthy person to be made.

If an ancient form of the Zika virus or any other kind of viral strain did in fact exist within the genetics of such species such as

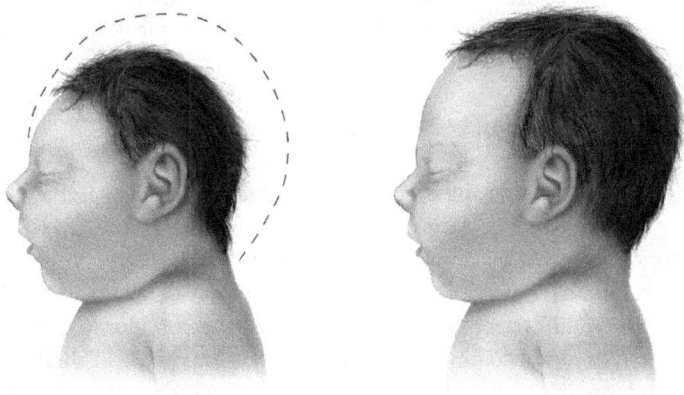

Homo Naledi and Homo Floresiensis, then it is likely one of the contributing factors that led to their eventual demise. A side note of interest found in Biblical prophetic end times books is that as the return of Jesus approaches; one major prophetic sign will be the outbreak of pestilence. Ezekiel 5:17 KJV states, *"So will I send upon you famine and evil beasts, and they shall bereave thee: and pestilence and*

*blood shall pass through thee; and I will bring the sword upon thee, I the Lord have spoken it."* Pestilence is defined as a deadly of virulent epidemic disease. Ezekiel 5:17 is an interesting scripture to consider for the modern world due to the outbreak and spreading of the Zika virus around the world during 2016 and the devastation it caused.

Tsz-Nephilimus Sapien was a hybrid species with several unique genetic factors. The large height and strength factors that were apparent in the species could have led to the overall genetic variables that, while not all at once, would eventually lead to the downfall of all other species of humanity save for Homo Sapiens. The long life expectancy of Tsz-Nephilimus Sapiens and their later descendants most certainly was affected by the changes to the environment. Certain traits would most likely become dormant or become recessive if those traits were not necessary for a later generation to use in an environment that was different than what previous traits would be helpful to in the species. However, if a species had interbred with other species before an actual extinction of the more pure bloodlines took place, then some of the original genetic material would no doubt survive.

Many anthropologists suggest that the brain evolves with the advancement in the evolution of a species towards a new generation. However, with discoveries into other human and other primate species such as Pithecanthropus (discovered on the island of Sumatra) led to the size of brains (pithecanthropus had a brain two-thirds the size of a Homo-Sapiens brain) in humans and apes that was smaller in size than in modern humans. This was believed to be the result of a lack of the growth of brain intelligence in the embryology stage of the brains development in later generations.

If we look at Homo-Sapiens along with Tsz-Nephilimus Sapiens as the forefathers of other human species, then one could make the claim that instead of the brains size growing or remaining smaller due to human advancement (or lack thereof) to our current level of intellect that the brain's size was due to the transference of viruses, diseases, genetic abnormalities, and other factors into later generations due to one or many differences in the genetic drift from the original host parent that is Homo Sapiens. Early Homo Sapiens possibly possessed smaller brain's as well, but had strong rates of growth due to advancements in intelligence and mental functions.

It has been confirmed that several Neanderthal and Homo Sapiens throughout the world did in fact have sexual relations and produced hybrid offspring. Were we to conclude that some of those children were able to pass on their genes into another generation, then it is only logical to assume that at least some trace of the Neanderthals still exist in the humans of today. This would also explain how several giants and other humans of unique abilities were able to still look like their Tsz-Nephilimus ancestors, have their aging factors, strength, and become people of legend in history.

It is possible that not all Tsz-Nephilimus Sapiens and even there future descendants were not giants. I point this out for a very specific reason. That reason being every extinct human specimen discovered throughout the world is not completely similar to another of its kind. They share common characteristics, but all have unique qualities similar to what can be seen among modern Homo Sapiens populations.

It is likely that while giants existed in the world, there were multiple height variety factors to take into account that made each giant and other Tsz-Nephilimus Sapien species produced unique. It can further be theorized that many of them were born with characteristics that made them mighty not just by status of height, but rather abilities stemming from strength, speed, ferocity, intelligence, and feats no one else could accomplish.

Paying special attention to timelines before even the rise of civilizations with technological innovations such as irrigation and agriculture would point out humans with more specific sets of skills needed to survive as hunter-gatherers. The abilities that many extinct humans and Homo Sapiens such as Cro-Magnon man would have would be height, strength, speed, internal factors such as stronger and flexible bones, and slower aging as many people lived past the age of two hundred. These features would also inspire the rise of heroes and champions over the course of history.

33

People who would witness feats of heroism and bravery by people with extraordinary abilities has been accounted for in all nations of the world. Many stories and legends of heroes have been told and retold with many changes over time to the story. What can be agreed on in regards to stories of heroes is, depending on the possibility that the hero of a story existed or not, that they did have an origin. No matter how many changes happen to a story over time, there is always a beginning that first inspired the story of a hero. Every culture in the world has stories of men and women that involve feats of super humans. The most famous stories of super humans and their heroic feats come from the ancient Greeks.

# CHAPTER 3: HEROES & FOUNDERS

The world has always made heroes and legends of men and women of extraordinary abilities. A lot of times these people can become deified as a result of their popularity. The mentality behind such actions falls under the age-old saying of "might makes right." People who are depicted as mighty often become heroes, champions, and even gods in the eyes of common people. The histories of Europe and Asia are full of accounts of such mighty people.

If we looked at Greek history and mythology together, we would see that they are connected. One major point that connects the myths with the history of Greece is the people that come into being in Greek history. Every group of people from Athenians, Spartans, Molossians, and others claim an ancestral lineage to an ancient Greek mythological character. The Spartans claim that they descend from Heracles or Hercules in the Roman translation. The Athenians descend from Theseus who killed the Minotaur (half bull and half man). The Molossians claim to have descended from Achilles, who was the hero from the Iliad of Homer. The list goes on for the Greek city-states that claimed ancestry to a particular Greek hero. While each city-state had a patron god or goddess like Athens who worshipped the goddess Athena, or Rhodes who worshipped Apollo, the Greek people are identified not with gods, but heroes of old.

The difference between a god and a hero is considerable. Pretty much the gods stayed up on Mount Olympus (located in the Balkans), demanded worship, and really didn't do anything else except bark orders at the people that paid tribute to them. The heroes on the other hand, were always busy with some kind of major issue or problem that only they could handle. The heroes of ancient Greece were often called demigods (a term also used in Mesopotamia, Persia, and other parts of Asia). The definition of a demigod is either a being with partial or low level divine (deity) status, or a man (or woman) who is greatly admired or respected. Another word for demigod is the Latin word *semideus* meaning half-god. A demigod is also used to describe Roman emperors such as Julius Caesar, who was declared a demigod by the Roman senate after winning a battle at Thapsus (an ancient city in modern day Tunisia). We can clearly see the title of a semi-divine being is bestowed upon someone by adoration, political declaration, or by popular election.

The Bible makes known the association of Tsz-Nephilimus Sapiens and their descendants with heroes and mighty men in two scriptures. The first scripture is Genesis 6:4 KJV, "*There were giants in the earth in those days; and also after that, when the sons of God came in unto the daughters of men, and they bare children to them, the same became mighty men* (heroes) *which were of old, men of renown.*"

The second is Psalms 89:6 KJV, "*For who in the heaven can be compared unto the Lord? Who among the sons of the mighty can be likened unto the Lord.*" The use of the word mighty is essential in these two scriptures. The definition of the word mighty is possessing great and impressive strength including on the account of size. Many of the ancient Greek heroes and figures are called mighty. The top fifteen of the Greeks mightiest heroes are Achilles, Heracles, Jason, Odysseus, Perseus, Theseus, Hector, Prometheus, Aeneas, Orpheus, Bellerophon, Pandora, Psyche, Phaethon, and Pasiphae. Many of these men from this list of fifteen are the sons of Greek gods.

The way to study the ancient heroes of mythology to possibly conclude them being real people is to break down the myths with factual evidence. In order to accomplish a study of this kind requires looking past tall tales told about certain characters and seeing if they can be attributed to real life accounts in history. Archaeological evidence of the places that heroes came from having even a fraction of truth to back up what they did there, such as performed some great feat there, fought a war there, or formed a civilization and gave rise to a people or population with a bloodline dating back to them needs to be proven. Finally, an anthropological approach using science to see if the physical and physiological traits of some of these heroes need to happen.

Some of the greatest empires and civilizations of history give account to having a lineage dating back to a mythological figure. Three Greek characters are identified with great civilizations of Greek and Italian history. For example, Theseus is the founder of Athens, and Heracles is the founder of Sparta. The biggest of these ancient heroes in connection to a great people would be Aeneas. Aeneas is a hero in Greek, Trojan, and Roman cultures. He is a Trojan by birth that escaped from the destruction of Troy following a ten-year war between the Greeks and the Trojans (which the Greeks won due to the Trojan horse deception). Being one of the few survivors of Troy and its destruction, Aeneas leaves his homeland (in modern day Turkey), heads to Italy, and establishes the society that would eventually become known as the Roman Empire.

According to the *Aenid* by the famed Roman poet and (my personal opinion) historical teacher due to his poetry being considered Didactic (educational and instructive), and Augustan (political poetry during the Augustan poetry movement); poet Publius Vergilius Maro or Virgil was the ancestor of the brothers Romulus and Remus, the founders of the Roman Republic. Aeneas is considered a progenitor of the ideals, beliefs, religious practices, laws, and culture that Rome would adopt and mold for their own way of life. This is seen in modern cultures from such places as China where medical doctor and political leader Sun Yat-sen (1866-1925) became the progenitor for both the Chinese Communist Party called the Peoples Republic of China (PRC), and the Chinese Nationalist Party called the Kuomintang (KMT) of China and later Taiwan.

Civilizations and cultures often begin with an individual who uses a single idea to spark the beginnings of a society. Romulus and Remus established the Roman Empire after not wanting to wait for the city of Alba Longa. Alba Longa was their grandfather's city in Italy that he ruled and was theirs by birthright. After his death it was to be turned over to them by legal inheritance. The brothers decided to create and entirely new city known as Rome. The brothers unfortunately squabbled over the location of Rome, which resulted in the death of Remus. Romulus founded Rome, created a senate, and formed the army or legions of Rome. Romulus himself would be mysteriously killed (some say disappeared but killed is more likely as most of the killings in Roman history were tied to political motivations) a few years later following the establishment of Rome's dominance, and Romulus becoming an autocratic leader in a democratic republic.

Roman civilization was heavily influenced by Trojan culture. The uniforms created for the Roman military were inspired by Trojan battle armor. The gods and deities of Rome were created from the Trojan religion brought to Italy by Aeneas. The wars and hostilities that would occur between Rome and Carthage (located in modern day Tunisia) originated from earlier wars between Carthage and Troy, and between Carthage and Aeneas himself when he launched a few more campaigns against Carthage while in Italy. Aeneas is an interesting character. A Trojan by birth, Aeneas was the son of a human prince named Anchises and a Greek goddess known as Aphrodite (Venus to the Romans). Aphrodite is the Greek goddess of love and beauty. He was a member of the Trojan royal family as the first cousin of king Priam, the father of the Trojan princes Hector and Paris. The hybrid status of Aeneas made him a demi-god, or a mighty man.

It is not impossible to assume that Aeneas existed. Mankind has only scratched the surface of the entirety of its history, and those who have lived in it. People don't realize that behind every society, civilization, culture, and empire is always one great figure that helped shape or plant the foundations of what would arise from them. Nazi Germany, for example, was ruled and molded by Adolf Hitler, and Fascist Italian leader Benito Mussolini inspired Hitler himself to mold Germany into another kind of Italy.

Hitler was also inspired by the members of the Thule Society that helped fund his campaign to become chancellor of Germany, and gave him the inspirations for the beliefs in German superiority from tales of myth and legends that he would pass onto the German people after the hardships Germany had endured following World War I. Mussolini himself was said to be Hitler's idol, as Mussolini sought to rebuild the Roman Empire and reclaim Italian might. This was the main reason for the emblem or standard of an eagle that Mussolini used as Italy's symbol during his reign as dictator.

Rome was not the only empire that would claim ancestry to Troy. Alexander the Great believed in the superiority of the Trojan culture. Alexander himself wore Trojan armor that he had acquired in Turkey during his campaigns against the Persian Empire. The Persian Empire claimed an ancestral lineage all the way back to Troy. So, we have the Roman Empire, the Macedonian Empire, and the Persian Empire all claiming a lineage to Troy. While Aeneas did not obviously influence Persia and Macedonia as he lived in Italy, the ideals he planted to begin the Roman Empire arose from the culture that he had fled from after its destruction at the hands of the Greeks. The honor of influencing all three major empires would fall to an individual who founded the very foundation of Trojan society. His name was Dardanus.

Dardanus was the son of Zeus and Electra, one of the seven daughters of the Titan Atlas who was cursed to hold up the sky for all time. He left Greece after Zeus murdered his brother over a woman (typical in Greek mythology); headed to where modern day Turkey is situated, and established a city called Troad. Dardanus would then have a son named Erichthonius; a king of a people called the Dardanians, and became the richest of men (as he is referred). He would then have a son named Troas who would found a city called Ilium, later to be called Troy. Two cultures would in fact be created from Dardanus. The first would be the Trojans by Troas, and the second would be the first people of the Dardanians who would be ruled by Troas brother Assaracus. The Dardanians would develop into the modern countries of Serbia, Kosovo, and part of northern Macedonia.

The reason for the mention of all of these cultural lineages is to show that everyone comes from a common single ancestor if you can look back far enough to see it. While many histories are controversial with only so much evidence to refer to and learn from for a common link, there is always a beginning somewhere in history that shows where everybody comes from. Whether or not those discoveries are true is to be determined by the truths, facts, and evidence discovered that are revealed by studying those findings.

Matthew 16:26 KJV says, "*For what is a man profited, if he shall gain the whole world, and lose his own soul? Or what shall a man give in exchange for his soul?*" All the people of the world and its civilizations are built on the beliefs of single or multiple individuals. For many descendants, the wisdom and knowledge of a patriarch or a progenitor are often reshaped or remade to fit the needs of a new generation of people. It is the way of things to change with the ever-flowing passage of time. If things don't change, then people wither and die. The people of Sparta are an example of this changing of ideals to fit a new generation by way of their claims to have descended from Heracles.

In the movie 300, the narrator of the story (played by David Wenham) makes a statement in the last scene of the battle of Thermopylae. He states that the Spartans are said to be descended directly from Heracles himself. Outside of the movie when the royal family of Sparta is traced back in history, there is one individual who many say was related to Heracles symbolically as the embodiment of the virtues of Heracles in the forms of law, and in the literal sense as a physical descendant. That man's name is Lycurgus.

Lycurgus was a lawgiver in Sparta. He created the military oriented reformation that completely overhauled Spartan society into the militaristic (or fascist) society that Sparta became known as in today's history. Lycurgus made three main community and military methods of reform in Spartan society. They were equality among the citizens, the fitness of the military, and austerity or attitude of sternness. Lycurgus is an interesting character for two reasons. First, he is not officially known to have existed, yet is referred to by many of the top historians and philosophers such as Herodotus, Plato, Plutarch, and Xenophon.

The Spartans are not often thought of in roles of diplomacy. Spartans are viewed for the military strategies. An interesting point of observation that eludes people is that the Spartans who were a fascist government nation lost the battle of Thermopylae. The Spartans are made famous for that battle due to standing against thousands of Persians with just an army of 300 Spartans and a few smaller rag tag Greek state military forces.

It was the Athenians in truth, who were a democratic state that won their naval battle against the Persians with a similar small sized force or fleet at the battle of Salamis. Lycurgus, however, is a Spartan known for government and therefore shows the Spartans did have political strength through more refined individuals of their culture.

A second point about Lycurgus is he and his family claim to be descendants of Heracles. Heracles is the ancestor of Lycurgus through the royal family lineage of Thespius. This claim goes back to an episode in Heracles life referred to humorously as the 13th labor. Heracles allegedly had sex with the daughters of Thespius (about fifty princesses in total) one night after he got drunk and thought he was sleeping with the same woman over and over. It is through this one night of multiple sexual episodes that the Spartans claim their ancestry to Heracles through the royal family, and by way of some non-family princesses of other houses that would make up other Spartan bloodlines. Lycurgus' lineage is traced back to Thespius who was the father of the princesses that Heracles impregnated, and thus carried on the royal line from him and the Spartan princesses or Dorian (the people the Spartans descend from) princesses and others from which Thespius would found Sparta.

The connection between Heracles and Lycurgus falls under the question of where the proof is that these two men existed? One man, Heracles, is a myth out of whom many people and beliefs came to be inspired and develop cultures and laws around. Lycurgus is another man whose existence is in question, yet is considered the original founder of Spartan society. How do we determine if these two legends were in fact real and blood related? The answer is not difficult but can be rather long. Let us break down the ways of identifying false from truth through five identification theory steps.

*Photos of Lycurgus Courtesy of C. Paul Jennewein (left picture) and Magnus Manske (right picture)*

1. Identify the founders and progenitors of cities, nations, civilizations, cultures, peoples, and other areas such as religions and movements.
2. Research the founding of bloodlines and family histories to see if there is even an inkling of possible connection to a figure or myth.
3. See what possible timeline in which the character of interest could have existed. It is important to realize some people may have existed in such times as the Paleolithic era instead of the Neolithic era.
4. Figure out from where the people actually came. For all we know certain people may not have even been from a culture such as Greece, but instead came from Hittite or Nubian cultures.

5. **Keep an open mind and always pay attention to every detail. No matter how small or benign something may be. The clue to discovery may be revealed in a detail you only recently noticed.**

The use of these five study tips will help anyone come to a better understanding of lineage. It is important to realize that many cultures that became great societies were not all built into glorious city-states and empires over night. The old saying of how Rome wasn't built in a day is totally true. The earliest cities and cultures developed out of the Stone Age.

Every place throughout the world has origins dating back to a group of people that slowly built themselves up from cave dwellers and mound builders into brick layers and metallurgists. When I was a kid I would often go to Disney World's Epcot Center and ride Spaceship Earth. I consider that ride my favorite because of the story it would tell about how mankind would first hunt together, then learn to speak a common language together in caves and later create complex societies complete with laws, literature, art, and written and spoken languages. That image will always remain with me as it showed me everyone came from somewhere small, but with effort and hard work grew bigger and greater over time.

One of the most important aspects of history that many people neglect is that a society often rose from the early or late Stone Age. People gathered together in small or large tribes, worked together to feed each other, protected one another from predators, and learned how to build a community through communication and sharing of information. No longer isolated or alone but striving together brought about what would turn into a society from tribal beginnings and eventually into a civilization. What also would come from the Stone Age beginnings are the many stories of heroes who performed such amazing feats that gave them a public standing as an icon of inspiration or deity type status that would be worshipped and have cults formed around them due to their heroic deeds and contributions to society.

# CHAPTER 4: PREDATORS AND CAVEMEN

The first appearance of man on the face of the earth was during the Pleistocene Epoch about 1.8 million years ago. This timeline included both the Ice Age and the Stone Age. Mankind had not yet evolved into the sophisticated social creature that it would one day become in the era of cities and roads. According to the first chapter of Genesis, man started out by spreading (migrating) all over the earth. Mankind was then given authority over the earth and animals.

Adam and Eve likely were plant and meat eaters. Fruit and vegetables are very important to a human's nutritional needs, but they can only satisfy so much of the human diet. Animals in the early Pleistocene Epoch were ferocious and timid. Many of the later species of such animals such as the horse and cow had ancestors in the same timelines that mankind was domesticating which could be classified as animals that would be able to become animals for food and societal needs.

What would make this connection to ancient Greek heroes such as Heracles falls under two distinct observations. The first is the clothing of Heracles, and the second being his height. Heracles was said to be over fifteen feet tall. He is often depicted wearing a lion's mane or head that he took from a beast called the Nemean lion of Nemea. The skin of the lion was said to be invulnerable to anything such as swords, arrows, and spears. Heracles killed the beast by basically ripping its head off with his bare hands. The Nemean lion also plays a part in figuring out if Heracles might perhaps be a figure from the Stone Age such as a shaman.

The Nemean lion is described as a beast with an indestructible skin and claws that could rip through metal. It is also depicted as a huge sized cat in artwork. Lions in Greece were common around 480 BCE (before the common era), then became endangered in 300 BCE, and became extinct in 100 BCE. Many lions in Europe were like today's African lions. However, prehistoric lions in Europe were much different than lions that we see today.

The most common prehistoric lion in Europe would be the Panthera Leo Fossilis, also called the Early Middle Pleistocene European Cave Lion. These lions grew to be about 2.4 meters or 7.9 feet in body length. Cave lions were about as big as the extinct American lion that existed in the Upper Pleistocene epoch. While many of the fossil bones have been recovered from the early Middle Pleistocene epoch, the European Cave Lion is best identified in terms of behavior, strength, and hunting prowess with that of its cousin Panthera Leo Spelaea, better known as the Eurasian Cave Lion. Both of these lions are identified as lions, but are also considered distinct subspecies of lions. They are sometimes considered in their own right a complete separate species called Panthera Spelaea due to the comparison of their skulls looking quite similar to tiger skulls rather than lions. However, genetic testing has kept the Cave Lion in the lion's category due to the similar genes they share with modern lions.

The Cave Lion was known as the biggest, smartest, and toughest of all the big cats, and one of the most dangerous of animals in its era. Cave lions were also among the largest cats ever to walk the earth. They were far larger than their cousins the Siberian Tigers of the modern world. Cave Lions lived during the Ice Age. They had a length ranging from 6 to 10 feet long. and had weights that varied from 100 to 1,000 pounds. Usually considered a single hunter, the Cave Lion may have hunted in groups or prides like modern day lions in order to take down large animals. The prey the Cave Lions hunted were often very big mega fauna or large animals. Cave Lions, unlike other Saber Tooth Cats of the Ice Age, had strong teeth that could crush bone. Speed was also an advantage. Cave Lions could move rapidly to capture prey thanks in part to their bodyweight being light enough for their physical frame to support bursts of speed and agility.

Lions were among the most notorious of problems in the Bible for many civilizations. The mighty Assyrian Empire once dealt with a plague of lions that God sent against them for not helping deal with Israel. Many murals of lions being hunted and killed by charioteers and kings are found in museums and archaeological pieces today. While not Cave Lions, the sheer size and physical might of the Asian Lions that the Assyrians had to deal with several

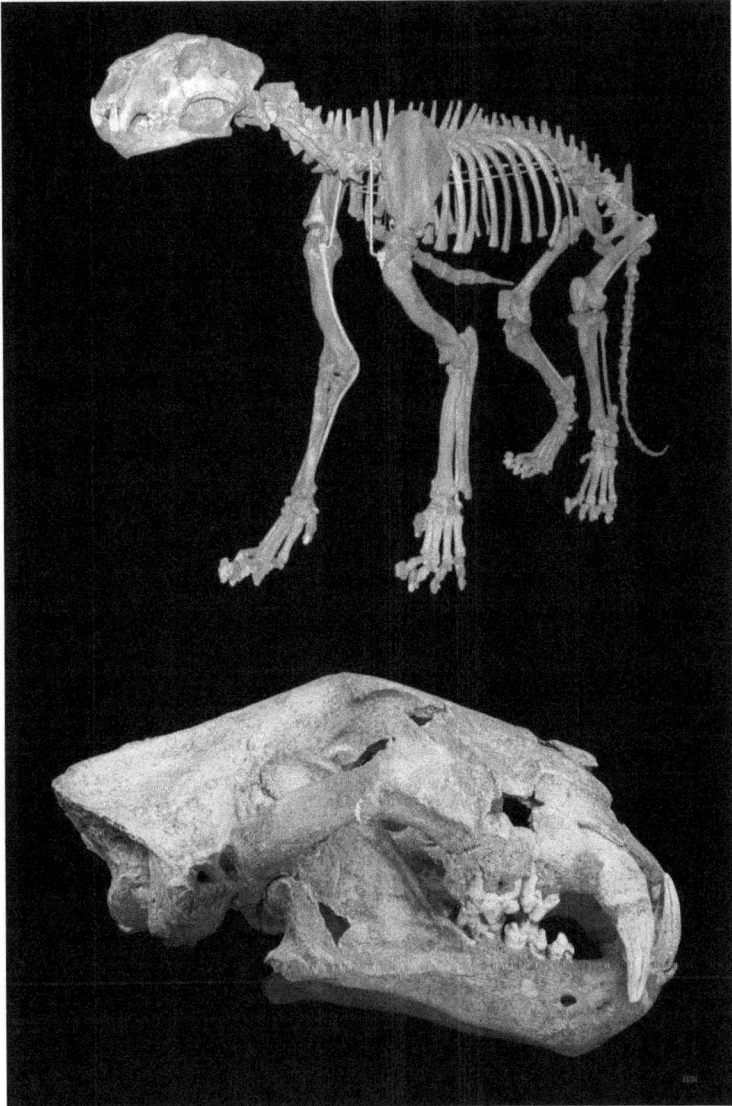

*Panthera Leo Spelaea or Cave Lion Courtesy of Tommy From Arad and
Didier Descouens*

thousand years ago can be seen as a glimpse of what the even older
and formidable Cave Lion would be like.

Cave Lions had a unique trait in their teeth.   As feline

carnivores, the Cave Lion possessed what is called Carnassial Shears. Carnassial Shears are two flat rear teeth between the fourth upper premolar and the lower first molar that could slice past each other like scissor blades. Like Hyenas who are identified as Felines (cats or similar to cats) instead of the usual belief that they are K-9s (dogs or dog relatives), Cave Lions also possessed molars that can crack bones from point-to point instead of crushing them. According to fossil records these lions possessed a powerful bite. With a strong enough bone structure and density, the teeth of a Cave Lion may have been strong enough to rip through early metal and armor.

The claws of a Cave Lion are different than their teeth. Claws are not bone as many people believe. They are part of the integumentary system, and are made of keratin, which is a tough protein that also makes up human fingernails. This makes claws homologous structures. Certain species can have highly developed bone structures near the claws. If the complexity of the bone is very highly developed, then the bone attachments will allow for a holding strength of great force for the claws when grabbing onto things. Like blades such as knives and swords, claws can become dull over time and therefore need to be sharpened. Depending on how sharp the lions could make their claws, it is likely that a well-sharpened claw could do serious damage against metal.

Aside from the sharpness and grip strength of a claw, another factor to take into consideration is the strength at which a lion swipe could be when it connected with a target. African Lions possess enough force in a swipe of their paw to crush the chest of a man. While certain factors are important to consider in such an attack, such as position of the swipe, armor, and even weight distribution can lead to the conclusion that if a modern lion has that kind of force in one paw swipe, just imagine the power of an ancient lion. Something like an 8 foot long, 700 to 800 pound Cave Lion's paw swipe would be to its prey like a sledge hammer smashing plate glass.

Many of the animals from prehistoric times pretty much went extinct right up to the end of the Ice Age, and the beginning of the Neolithic age. However, there is always a possibility of a few, to at least one, sole survivor of a species that could still exist even after the majority of the species has all but died out. This is the beauty and genius of genetics. While many scientists aspire to the ideology of natural selection, they often forget about the probability of random mutation. If a species begins to die out, then the chances of *survival of the fit,* the original phrase terminology before it was changed to *survival of the fittest,* will most possibly come into play. It is possible that the Nemean Lion may have been a Cave Lion or a last known descendant or hybrid spawn of another species of European lion mixed with a Cave Lion.

Heracles fought and killed the Nemean Lion in a cave by strangling it to death. After this, Heracles skinned the lion with his own claws and wore the skin as armor, and as a trophy. Cave Lions do not have manes. However, the stories of Heracles don't say that he wore a lion's mane, but the skin of the beast. Skin was a common used form of clothing among cave men. While many of the clothes are for practical use such as warmth and protection, some animal skins were worn as forms of authority and adoration. This is a common practice among many peoples. Romans 1:22-23 ESV reads, *"Claiming to be wise, they became fools, and exchanged the glory of the immortal God for images resembling man and birds and animals and creeping things."*

Many sites of Paleolithic civilizations in Greece like the settlements of Dimini and Sesklo showed great development by 3000 BCE. Possibly many of those peoples used animal heads and skins in their worship of animals, elements, and people (possibly such as Heracles) by Shamans and tribal chiefs. Heads of lions, wolves, bears, and other great animals were common clothing for many men and women of importance in the Stone Age. Heracles might have adopted that practice when he wore the Nemean Lion's skin as an article of clothing. The fact he was often pictured naked with only the skin of the Nemean Lion on his head portrays both the ancient Greek mentality of nude figures and displays of manhood and womanhood, and a possible caveman idea as many ancient humans did not wear full articles of clothing.

*\* Caveman with Deer Headdress (Left) Courtesy of Benjamin D. Esham and Heracles with Nemean Lions Skin Headdress Courtesy of Jastrow*

Cavemen such as Neanderthals and Cro-Magnon (a Homo Sapiens next stage of development into more complex social groups and individuals) wore animal skins as sources of warmth and protection. They wore certain unique attire for other uses such as leadership and religious reasons. In prehistoric days there were many locations that today are considered religious or occult sites for certain groups of animal deity worship. There were many cults back in the Stone Age that were based around animal worship. When Heracles came on the scene in ancient Greece, many cults surrounding him were created. Deification is based around making something into an image of worship by way of how it impresses people to make them want to worship whatever it is they choose to make into an idol. For many ancient human species it was animals.

For modern Greeks and others, it was Heracles. Had Heracles himself been impressed by the Nemean Lion possibly would explain why he chose to wear the lion's skin on his body. While I am not saying he worshipped the beast he killed, perhaps he felt it was a mark of honor to wear the skin of the beast he killed as some rite of passage. The practice of marking oneself with the blood of a kill, the wearing or use of something from after death, or the drinking of an animals blood after it had been killed are practices that have been around for eons as ways to show off a trophy, gain power and prestige, or to show respect to the creature by portraying them on the body of the one who killed it.

Determining whether or not Heracles is actually an individual from prehistoric times is difficult due to the lack of evidence to support the theory. However, we have to realize that all myths spring from a single story that over time can keep having things added to them in order to make them more interesting and entertaining. If we were to say that Heracles was a giant of 15 feet tall, and had an amazing strength factor, then perhaps he could have been a cave man as many other caveman species in the Ice and Stone Age possessed impressive strength, aging, and other attributes.

We can factor in that the feats and unity that Heracles would bring to the people that saw him do these feats, heard him speak about, and took inspiration from would no doubt have people try and incorporate into their own codes, ethics, honor, laws, and religious practices. That way they could use a mighty figure that displayed virtues of a civic nature and turn them into the pillars of what would ultimately become a future society, and maybe even a nation. It would also give rise to the religious and cultic practices that would stem from the obvious worship and deification of such an individual like Heracles that societies do create.

Many people themselves have been the inspiration for mythical figures as a whole. Amazons, Centaurs, Sirens, and other groups of figures have their origins in actual people. The Scythians of Asia are among the inspirations for Centaurs and Amazons in Greek mythology (as well as possibly other Asian legends and myths). In the next chapter we will explore the rise of the Scythians throughout the ages from them as horsemen of the Black Sea, to their rise as alleged ancestors of legendary British King Arthur and his knights of the Round Table of Camelot.

# CHAPTER 5: SCYTHIANS AND AMAZONS

All great walks of life begin from different steps. When going into the history of Asia's many cultures and great civilizations beginnings, there is one group of people that are said to have been the founders of many nations ranging from China, India, Russia, and others in Europe such as the Slavic peoples and Norsemen. That unique group is not a nation, but rather a confederation of tribal or Nomadic horsemen and women known as the Scythians.

The word *Scythian* is a Greek work along with several other words used to identify them such as *Scythe* due to the fact no one knows the original name since the Scythians were illiterate and never wrote down their actual name. Other names for the Scythians are *Saka* from Old and New Persian (pronounced differently in both tongues but spelled the same), Sacae in Latin, and Sai in Chinese.

The Scythians were a group of people who lived and inhabited large areas around the Eurasian Steppes, which were landmasses of both Asia and Europe commonly called Eurasia. They existed from the 9th century BC until the 1st Century BC. In 100 BC the Scythians literally vanished from history with only a few theories as to what happened to them. They spoke tribal languages that are similar in speech to Eastern Iranian branch languages, and were not literate (could read and write). They used pictograph forms of storytelling and history keeping. The Scythians existed in Central Asia as a group called the Iskuzai or Askuzai. At times, they were called Scytho-Siberians due to the areas and kingdoms they left behind in Siberia.

The Scythians were great riders and breeders of horses. Their whole culture centered on riding and ownership of horses. They were masters of a military style of warfare called mounted warfare or horseback warfare. Being a nomadic group from the Steppes which are montane grasslands in and around the lower regions of Russia and surrounding areas such as Mongolia, Kazakhstan, and Ukraine, mounted warfare suited the Scythians as it did other nomadic tribes who were often in conflict with one another. Nomadic life was perfect for warfare in Scythian horsemen culture. Steppe warfare produced potent military forces such as cavalry.

The fighting potential of the nomadic tribes was often limited due to the number of individuals that would make up a nomad army, and unity was rare among tribes as only on occasion did two or more tribes work together to defeat a common enemy. However, once in a while a strong leader would rise up, and then many tribes would work together as a massive fighting force that would basically be unstoppable. Such unity was rare, but did occur if in the eyes of the tribes the leader was worthy of diverse loyalty, and intertribal war bound (conscripted to a common struggle) armies.

The Scythians were powerful fighters and warriors. Their technology for horsemanship is believed to be some of the first real innovations that would be adapted for later horseback riding. Trousers were attributed to the Scythians as they are depicted in art of war and trade pictures wearing them on and off their horses similar to how a cowboy wore spurs and chaps when riding in the Old West. The Scythians fought with armor from head to toe, used lances, spears, swords, bows and arrows, and other weapons from mounted horseback. The Scythians possessed great skills as goldsmiths and metallurgists. Many of their gold art and ornaments are on display in museums in Russia and China.

The Scythians were a feared people. In the ages they lived where empires such as the Assyrians, Persians, and Medians ruled and fought with vast armies and superiority, the Scythians were one people these empires never wished to pick a fight against. Persian incursions often occurred into Scythian territory, and usually the

Persians were sent home in body bags. The historian Herodotus once recorded a scuffle between the Persians and Scythians where the Persians were outmatched and outmaneuvered by the Scythians who knew the terrain and cartography (mapping) of the area that they were fighting in much better, and were relentless in their pursuit of the Persians who barely made it back into Persian territory alive. Scythians practiced brutal warfare tactics as well as cultural practices such as heavy drug use and full body tattooing.

The Scythians, aside from being brutal, were among the most formidable enemies of the Persian and Assyrian empires. It was the Scythians, with the aid of a few other nations such as the Cimmerians, that wiped out the Assyrian Empire around 615 BC. The elimination of the Assyrians was not all at once, but over a gradual period of time. The Scythians themselves (as previously mentioned), as a whole, vanished from history by 100 BC.

The Scythians were nomads of the Steppes. They could move and travel as they pleased with no limits to where they went. Many civilizations in Asia can be traced back to a Scythian lineage. Many cultures from modern day nations of India, Pakistan, China, Russia, and Iran all have some claims to Scythian ancestry. It is possible that many Western European peoples from Ireland and England have Scythian ancestry due to their migration into Western Europe. It is theorized that those same Scythians carried the sword of Goliath to Ireland, but that claim remains unconfirmed.

If we were to look at the interactions of the Greeks and other European peoples that were in contact with the Scythians, then the list would be enormous. Like the Huns of Asia that roamed all the way from China to Hungary, almost all the ancient peoples of Eastern Asia had a brief period of relationship, warfare, or trade dealings with the Scythians in the same manner. The Scythians were more than just a small group of tribes that put fear into the nations and empires around them. They were a confederation of tribes that could be unified under a common goal similar to the

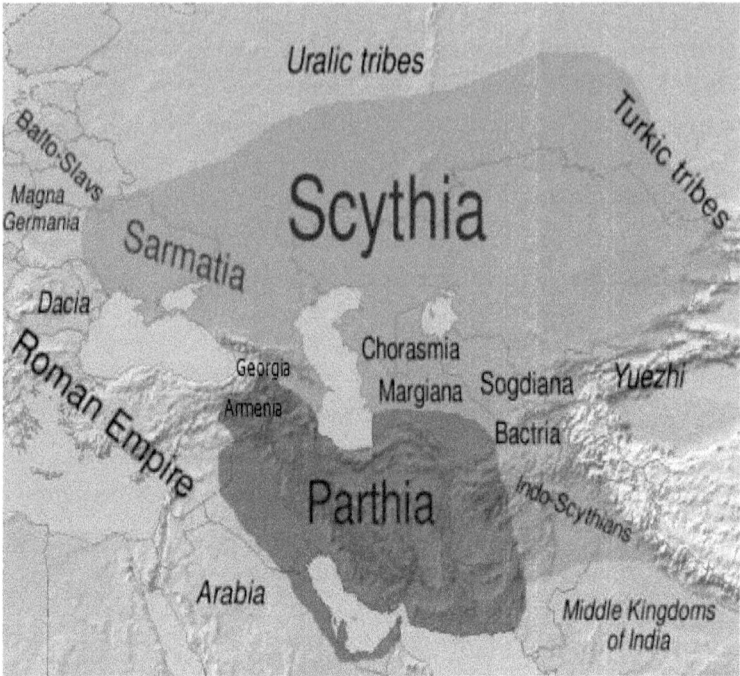

*Scythian Territory Courtesy of Dbachmann*

Native Americans of North America. They had art, culture, history, and traditions of trade and horse breeding that made them not only a warrior culture and society, but also a civilization.

The Scythians evolved from the Pazyryk culture that existed in the Altay region that existed from the 6th to 3rd centuries BC. The Pazyryk culture ranged from the Altay Mountains in Kazakhstan and nearby Mongolia. Today, the Pazyryk cultural area is located in the Republic of Altai, Russia. Like the Scythians that descended from them, the Pazyryk culture is considered to have embraced a war-like lifestyle.

Acts 17:26 KJV says, "*And hath made of one blood all nations of men for to dwell on all the face of the earth, and hath determined the times before appointed, and the bound of their habitation...*" The Scythians were a people that arrived just mysteriously as they would disappear in 100 B.C. There are many speculations as to where exactly the Scythians came from in the bowels of history. Two of the stories center around two connecting, possibly same origins that deal with a giant from ancient Greece named Typhon.

Accordingly to Greek mythology, Typhon was the son of Gaia (Earth) and Tartarus. Tartarus is a type of supermax prison section of Hell (Hades in Greek) for the Titans and other wicked creatures of Greek mythology. The mention of elements and locations as parents is interesting. Colossians 2:8 KJV reads, *"Beware lest any man spoil you through deceit, after the tradition of men, after the rudiments of the world* (elemental spirits of the world)\*, *and not after Christ."*

We can further see the mention of elemental spirits in Colossians 2:20 KJV, *"Wherefore if ye be dead with Christ from the rudiments of the world* (elemental spirits of the world)\*, *why, as though living in the world, are ye subject to ordinances."*[1]

Typhon is said in other stories to be born of Gaia, but not with Tartarus as his father. According to Greek tradition, Typhon could actually be the son of Hera, the wife of Zeus, who was sick and tired of Zeus' infidelity as he constantly cheated on her with earthly women and men and had Typhon out of anger with the assistance of Gaia. It is also stated that Hera had Typhon with Zeus' father, the Titan Cronus. Whatever the actual story may be, Typhon is a child that was produced out of spite, anger, hatred, resentment, and bitterness.

The results of Typhon's birth comes from the same principles that we are warned of from Galatians 4:3 KJV, *"Even so we, when we were children, were in bondage under the elements* (elementary principles)\* *of the world."*

---

[1] \* Is addition by author

This comes to further revelation in Galatians 5:19-21 KJV, *"Now the works of the flesh are manifest, which are these: Adultery, fornication, uncleanness, lasciviousness, idolatry, witchcraft, hatred, variance, emulations, wrath, strife, seditions, heresies, envyings, murders, drunkenness, revellings, and such like: of the which I tell you before, as I have also told you in time past, that they which do such things shall not inherit the kingdom of God."*

These types of earthly principles are a weakness that all mankind shares until they break them off through Christ and common sense. This is read in Galatians 4:9 KJV, *"But now, after that ye have known God, or rather are known of God, how turn ye again to the weak and beggarly* (worthless) *elements, where unto ye desire again to be in bondage?"*

Desires that are spawned from manners that are of negativity result in negative outcomes. A child born from such a negative desire can often embrace negativity and become the bane of existence that a parent feels when they become pregnant from such a principle they want to make a living reality or nightmare in this case.

Typhon is believed to be the last of a race of giants that were wiped out by the Olympian's gods during a war known as the Gigantomachy. He is thought to have been born in an area called Cilicia, found in modern day Kizkalesi, Turkey, in a cave known as the Cilician Cave(s). There is belief among many scholars that at one point many giants in fact lived in the area that would become the country of Turkey. Typhon is considered to be outrageous, terrible, and lawless. He is said to have been extremely strong, untiring, surpassed all the offspring of the earth or Gaia, and had features like a snake or dragon. He was described as emitting horrible sounds that were confusing and hard to listen to when heard. Typhon hated everything and everyone. Many of the descriptions of Typhon made him out to be multiple headed, snakelike, winged, and had fire in his eyes. Needless to say that

Typhon was not the kind of individual one would want to make an enemy of or meet in a dark alley.

Typhon was the number one challenger to Zeus in mythology for control of the cosmos. After a grueling and hellish battle, Typhon lost to Zeus. Typhon escapes at one point during the fight with Zeus to the Caucasus region, possibly to the Caucasus Mountains in Eurasia between the Black and Caspian Seas. These lands include what is today part of the nations of Turkey, Armenia, Azerbaijan, Georgia, Russia, and Iran. These would be the areas that the Scythians would occupy, migrate from place to place, and eventually settle to form their own culture and the cultures of many current nations of the modern world.

Typhon is a unique character among the Greeks. He and his wife Echidna (a half woman and half serpent creature similar to Hindu and Buddhist Nagas) are considered to be the father and mother of monsters. This is not necessarily too far a stretch when considered. If Typhon did exist, then it is possible that the people that would descend from him are the inspirations for the monsters he is claimed to have fathered similar to how the Scythians are associated with Centaurs and Amazons.

The Scythians are said to be the inspirations for the half horse and half man Centaurs and the legendary Amazonian women of Greek mythology. Scythian women were called Amazons in certain circles due to their status as fearless warriors. Women warriors where rare among Aryan or Indo-Iranian peoples. To the Greeks it was also a rarity for a woman to be a warrior. The women of the Scythians were very much like mixed martial artists and modern military women. They were strong, masculine, tattooed, fearless, and independent.

Scythian women were allowed to fight in cavalry positions along side men. They were allowed certain rights due to their warrior status, though a rare practice even among the Scythians as it still was an age were women were not looked at in favorable positions outside of home and baby makers. Scythian women had tattoos; many of them full sleeve tattoos, and could own a horse and be buried with it at death just like Scythian men. In one story of a tribe of the Scythians known as the Amyrgians, a joint force of 300,000 men and 200,000 Scythian women went to war with Cyrus the Great. That conflict ended favorably as the Scythians found Cyrus to be an honorable ruler to make peace with him and fight for him on occasion as Scythians acted every so often as mercenaries, or were conscripted to military service for Persia and a few other empires.

The Scythians had nobility and royalty. Many of their great tribal leaders were not merely chiefs, but kings. Among many of the archeological discoveries found in Kurgans (burial mounds), treasury rooms and other Scythian remains contained gold crowns, jewelry, and ornaments such as scepters, bowls, pottery, and early bong pipes for drug use and mixing cups for alcohol. The Scythian society was used to making their own art and having art made for them by such cultures as the Greeks. Without the interactions from the Greeks it is likely that the Scythians would not have become as famous in legend or for the inspiration of mythological creatures that would come from them.

The Centaur descriptions would most likely be due to the fact that the Scythians were masters of the horse. Scythians could shoot arrows perfectly from horseback. They could use a spear and lance from a mounted position with favorable accuracy. They were very effective at using shield and sword from the back of a horse. The thing that could put real fear of fighting the Scythians into a person was the utter relentless nature that the Scythians had when engaging an enemy. When an enemy entered their territory, the Scythians would literally hunt down every last intruder until they were caught. If the enemy was fortunate enough, they might die in combat with a Scythian. If an enemy got caught alive, then there was a good chance they would be executed as prisoners of

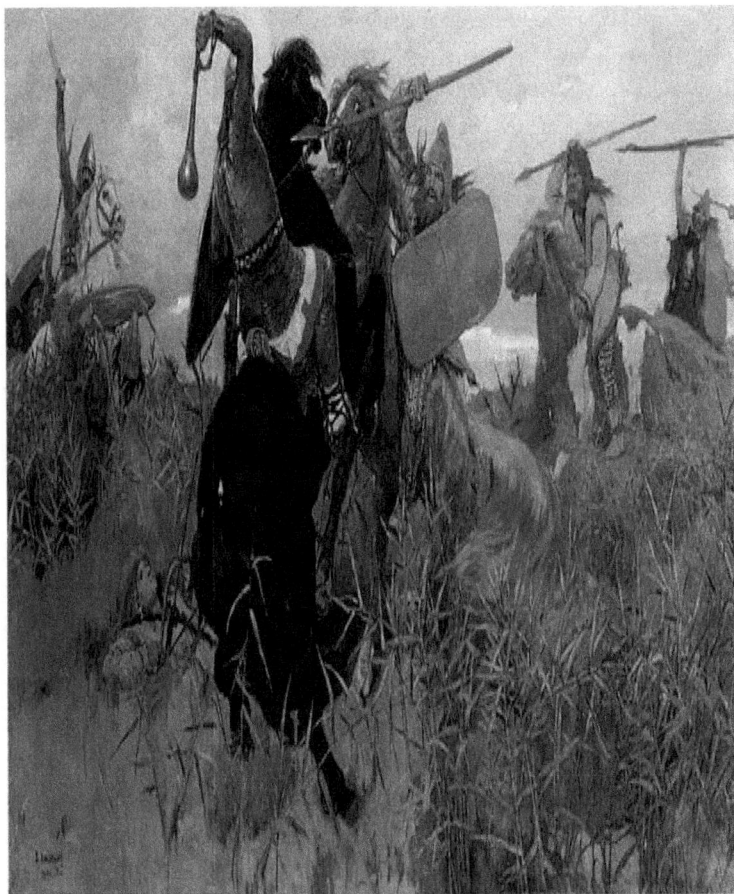

*Scythians (right) Against The Slavs By Viktor Vasnetsov in 1881.

war, or enemies of the state. Execution by Scythians could be brutal, as the Scythians were known for practicing barbarous methods of punishment and execution such as crucifixion and beheading.

Other traits that were similar between Centaurs and Scythians was that both the mythological Centaurs and the very real Scythians liked to party. Scythians and Centaurs liked to get hammered on alcohol, get stoned out of their minds or high as a kite (or both) on pretty much any recreational drug they chose to indulge in for any and all occasions. Scythians loved to get into trouble. While a tempered people that did interact with other cultures, the Scythians were first and foremost a warlike culture that loved to fight.

The Scythians appeared as large men at times in art and descriptions. Greek combs given to Scythian chiefs often show the men on horseback having legs that almost reached to the ground. While not all of them were giants, many of them were no doubt very tall and powerful individuals. The Scythians had several different physical characteristics such as being red-haired and grey eyed people, fair colored hair, green, hazel, and blue eyes, red haired with blue eyes, and blond-haired with light-eyes. They were all described as having ruddy skin, dark skin, and fair-skinned. It needs to be pointed out that many of these descriptions came from several historical sources such as Herodotus, Ammianus Marcellinus, and Galen (a physician) that spanned several different timelines, and several areas of Asia and Europe.

The main connections of the Scythians to other nations that they would help make the foundations for add a great contribution to the study of genetic drift. Even when a species dies out, there is always the possibility of some of their lifeblood existing in the genetics that may one day rise again in a new generation. Scythians possibly were the influence for the British legends of King Arthur and his Knights of the Round Table.

Two groups from Scythia that are believed to have migrated to what is now the United Kingdom are the Scythians and Sarmatians. Both are horsemen and people of the Steppes. Sarmatians are referred to as the Turkic knights of King Arthur due to their large cultural ties to the Turkish peoples that would one day occupy and make up what would become Turkey. However, it is more likely that the Scythians are the true knights and possibly King Arthur himself.

There is one story that sticks out about the migration patterns of the Scythians from the areas of the Black Sea towards Ireland. The story, while short, describes the Scythians taking the sword of Goliath all the way to Ireland where they would one day settle. The connection to the sword of Goliath is fascinating as the Scythians genetic connection to Tsz-Nephilimus Sapiens possibly could have some common ground with Goliath and the people from which he and his brothers came. While we know Goliath and his brothers were Philistines, we don't know the exact parental lineage of them except that they may have been cousins to King David.

According to the Babylonian Talmud, Goliath and his brothers were the sons of Ophar or Orpah, the sister of Ruth who was the great grandmother of King David. It is actually believed that both women were actually sisters as they are both considered daughters of King Eglon of Moab in the Bible. Eglon was a cruel and fat king who oppressed Israel until he was assassinated by the Israelite judge Ehud in Judges 3:21-22. Orpah and Ruth are often viewed as sister-in-laws in the Bible, but they are never called sister-in-laws. They are referred to as daughter-in-laws of Naomi, and the wives of Naomi's sons Mahlon and Chilion, but never as sister-in-laws. It is very likely they were in fact sisters by blood.

Orpah is identified by the name Harafa when mentioned in the lineage of Goliath as the name means threshing. She is considered to have had sex with several men similar to how wheat is threshed or harvested by trampling, pounding, or beating repeatedly. Harafa had her name changed to Orpah when she stayed behind in the land of Moab instead of going with her mother-in-law Naomi and Ruth to Judea as read in Ruth 1:13-16. The name Orpah in Hebrew definition means neck or fawn. The word fawn is defined as a young deer or a pretty young girl. The definition can also be further defined as one who has yet to be unweaned (unaccustomed to anything else).

The name Orpah is sometimes spelled Orpha. The secondary spelling of Orpha is identified with the Greek word Orphanos meaning orphan. Orphan is defined as one who has lost both parents by death, abandonment, disappearance, desertion, or separation by one or both parents. According to the story Naomi, Ruth, and Orpah when they were figuring out what to do next after the death of their spouses, Naomi basically said she did not want either daughter-in-law to go with her back to Judea. Orpah returned to her own people and gods, while Ruth went with Naomi to her people and her God. If we broke down the situation to simple terms, then we could consider Orpah as having thought that Naomi was abandoning her by not wanting her to go to Judea with her.

In a way, Orpah shares a similarity with the Scythians as they were people who never really settled for anything. The Scythians were nomads who wandered from place to place, never really belonging to anyone, and Orpah possibly never remarried again thus making her in a sense a sojourner in her own land as her family seemed to abandon her to find her own path in life. Orpah was born a Moabite woman, but she married into a Jewish family with different beliefs, customs, and a God different from her gods. Like Moses, she never really belonged anywhere as her life took so many different paths. Even though Orpah was born into a Moabite family, perhaps she never went back to them or they never accepted her back. With no father or mother, mother-in-law, sister, or husband Orpah truly could be identified as an orphan that was abandoned or deserted in her life.

One interesting extra point of observation on Orpah and the Scythians is that the Scythes worshipped a deer god in their religious beliefs. Much of their art and ornaments always were designed with depictions of deer's with beautiful ornamentation and reverence. With Orpah's name meaning fawn, it could very well be a coincidence, but perhaps there is a link somewhere between Orpah and the Scythians by way of their symbols and

*Scythian Gold Stag Courtesy of Daderot*

cultural beliefs. The story of the Scythians being in possession of the sword of Goliath is also an interesting connecting point as Orpah was the mother of Goliath. Though meager evidence, we see possible links between Orpah and the Scythians by what is revealed in stories and religion.

The parents of Goliath and his brothers have produced some possible connections between the Philistines and the Scythians. It is a confirmed fact that Scythians migrated all over Asia and Europe and established several societies. The idea of Scythians becoming legendary knights is not impossible to believe if enough evidence can be gathered to prove it. What can be shown is Scythians and Arthurian stories do contain great details of horsemen and great battles fought by both groups.

Scythians are also considered to be the people from whom Gautama Buddha descended in history. Gautama Buddha was the Buddha that founded Buddhism after leaving his life as a prince and attempting to seek enlightenment. Buddha was believed to have lived mostly in the eastern part of ancient India between the sixth and fourth centuries BCE. While only speculative, Buddhism does share many similarities to the Scythian religion of Assianism that is still practiced today by the Ossetians of modern Russia who are the only known descendants of the Scythians. Another interesting tidbit of information is that Kassapa Buddha, the predecessor to Gautama Buddha, was a giant of 20 cubits in height. The people from which the Buddhas come, the Saykas, are considered Scythians as they were described as foreign people who did not like Hinduism as they disrespected Brahmins, and even described one of the Buddhas as having blue eyes. Blue eyes were a common physical trait of Scythians but not ancient Indians.

The connection of Buddhism to the Scythians is one more piece of information that the Scythians had many interactions with different cultures. To assume they had links to Great Britain as knights and possible inspirations on the Arthurian legends isn't impossible when given careful consideration.

# CHAPTER 6: KNIGHTS & MOUNTED RIDERS

During my first year of university level education I was studying medieval literature and history. I took two important classes that tied the modern and ancient worlds together. Those classes were medieval history, and the history of World War II. What tied them together was a statement that my teachers made about Adolf Hitler and King Arthur Pendragon (King Arthur's real last name). According to my teachers, Adolf Hitler once read *The Once and Future King*, which was the English version of the King Arthur story or the Arthurian legends.

I found out that many of the great and worst leaders of history had read *The Once and Future King*. Having read the French version entitled *King Arthur's Last Battle,* a more condensed and concise version but with the same flare as the English version, I saw why many great leaders would read a story about knights, the Holy Grail, and mystical lands filled with wizards and dragons.

The story of King Arthur Pendragon is based on the achievements of a king who was appointed by divine authority. He rose through society and hierarchy by way of the sword and the pen (meaning politics and diplomacy), and established a government by knowing who to rub shoulders with among nobility and royalty. He would make war and peace, and would leave a lasting legacy before embarking on the adventures that awaited in death after a long and lengthy life. Every great leader has attempted to make such a life and legacy for themselves. The only difference between them and King Arthur is how they achieved or attempted to achieve their goals, as some leaders were very great, while others were very wicked.

The world of knights varies from place to place. The definition of knight for the modern age is an honorary title granted by a monarch or other political leader for services to leadership, country, or military merit. In ancient times, knights were a class of lower nobility. They represented codes of conduct, chivalry, and a moral example of a Christian or other type of religious warrior as was observed in the early and late Middle Ages. More than that, knights were mounted riders, which meant that they rode horses.

The ideas behind chivalry and codes of honor were simply dependent on if a knight chose to embrace such ideals. Knights were not men (and occasionally women) in shining armor. More often than not, knights were more like DC comics Batman who is usually referred to as the dark knight. Batman, while a fictional character, is portrayed as a man who believes in a code of honor and is deeply committed to them. Batman doesn't kill, but will literally use any other means and methods to accomplish his goals. He wears the symbol of a bat to inspire fear in his enemies just as bats frighten him. He wears high quality battle armor and uses state of the art weaponry and gadgets to do battle. He fights against the worst of humanity in order to protect the lives of others from the things that he encounters on a daily basis. While a fictional character, Batman carries the type of mystique that ancient knights embraced far more than the cutesy knight in shining armor critique that knights have become accustomed.

In my opinion, a knight is someone of deep convictions. Conviction is defined as a firmly held belief or opinion. The idea of a knight being a man or woman of conviction is dependent on what they chose to put their faith in that merits servitude. 2 Peter 3:16 ESV says, *"As he does in all his letters when he speaks in them of these matters. There are some things in them that are hard to understand, which the ignorant and unstable twist to their own destruction, as they do the other scriptures."* Knights of the ancient world often belonged to a particular faction or order.

*King Arthur, His Knights of the Round Table, and The Holy Grail*
*Courtesy of Evrard d'Espinques*

Following the fall of the Roman Empire, knightly orders

appeared over almost all of Europe.

Knights existed in other parts of the world. Some were not called knights, but in a sense were knights based on their similar lifestyles to European knights. One such group was the cavalrymen of Bornu, who rode and terrorized the area of what is now central Sudan. Operating through the 16th century, the Bornu knights would go on yearly marches against weaker people to keep themselves in fighting shape. The Bornu cavalry (or Bornu Knights as I call them) wore coats of mail composed of iron chain that covered them from head to toe. They rode richly caparisoned horses that could move with great precision and expertise of the finest horse qualities.

Named the Negro knights by the British, the cavalry of Bornu made the British in 1823 proclaim them to have knightly courtesy mixed with defiant pride. They were known to greet the British with courteous gestures that had an aura of defiance in them. The mention of the Bornu knights is to show that knights are not just apart of Europe's great historical culture, but are found in places on other continents with warriors that either had the same flair of European knights, or who were referred to as knights by the peoples of Europe.

The origin of knights comes from their history as mounted riders. A mounted rider was one who rode a horse. Cavalry were mounted riders. Cavalry riders were what allowed Alexander the Great to defeat the mighty Persian Empire and conquer much of the known world. The mounted riders of the Huns were the nightmare of the Roman Empire as they made such advances against the empire that had history unfolded differently might have had an emperor Attila (ruler of the Hunnic Empire) of Rome in history.

Mounted riders were among the most unique of military in the ancient world. They could cover great distances in short time. They could fight from an elevated position (horseback) with sword, spear, javelin, lance, bow and arrow. They would wear battle armor, as would their horse that would allow them to take damage from foot soldiers and other mounted riders and continue fighting. A mounted rider would be a harder target for an archer to hit as they could be moving at increased speeds, and with (certain riders wearing) well enforced armor would allow a rider to be able to fight more efficiently than a soldier on foot.

The most effective horsemen could be more fearsome and effective in battle than a chariot. Chariots were effective as early tanks because soldiers from a chariot could shoot arrows, throw spears, slash with swords, or simply trample or cut down opponents as some chariots had long rods protruding from a chariot wheel that could cut down or slice up an opponent. Soldier's unfortunate enough not to move out of a chariots path usually met a gruesome end.

A mounted rider could move behind a chariot and attack the openings available, as chariot drivers (charioteers) would be more focused on what was going on in front and to their sides. Mounted riders could shoot arrows, throw spears, or hurl javelins from their mounts (horses) at a similar to equal height of a chariot on certain terrain. Mounted riders would even have better maneuverability on a single horse as opposed to a large chariot that would require more time and space to turn properly. This is what gave the Scythians, Cimmerians, Sarmatians, Huns, and other horse cultures of Asia, Europe, and Africa advantages over the great empires of the old world.

One final point of interest involving the Scythians is one particular sacred site to them. Mount Caucasus, located between the Black Sea and Caspian Sea, is called a Scythian mountain. Mount Caucasus is believed to be the prison of the Titan Prometheus who was punished for giving fire to mankind. The Scythians believed in mountain spirits, and according to some beliefs, thought the mountains had spirits and demons in the rocks. It is likely that the Caucasus Mountains were sacred to the Scythians in a way that is similar to the way the Amorites considered mountains sacred (to be covered more in section two). The Greeks who lived along the Black Sea and Caucasus Mountains made claims that Heracles was in fact the father of the Scythian people similar to the way the Spartans claim ancestry to Heracles. The mention of that fact is to show that the Scythians have many strong ties to possible giant origins in their beginnings as a people.

Scythians may have been the ancestors that would establish the later peoples of Western Europe. They also established the next generations of peoples in China, Russia, India, Pakistan, and other places throughout Asia. The Scythians possibly came from a combination of the peoples of Greece and Asia by way of what is now modern Turkey. The Greeks and the Scythians did have relations by ways of trade and cultural interactions such as through art and the occasional treaty (the Scythians were in continual conflict with the empires of Assyria and Persia as did the Greeks).

Aside from the Scythians, there are older cultures and places that reveal many mysteries to us that are studied through archaeology. In the next section of the book we will go into detailed information about much older cultures that can help connect the dots to many places, societies, and civilizations that will help further explain more of the widespread influence of Tsz-Nephilimus Sapiens and their origins.

There is a need to dig into the history of the cultural practices of the rise of a society. The tribal origins of people are one of the keys to discovering true facts of history. The Bible has scriptures that use phrases such as "before time" that can be found in Deuteronomy 2:12, and further wording to identify timelines marked by names of leaders in association with the land such as "the land of Rameses" found in Genesis 47:11 that connects to the 430 year timeline that the Israelites were in Egypt as citizens and later slaves. If Stone Age Biblical roots can be studied, archaeology can reveal more intimate details to connect the dots that history and theology have hidden away that would help shed more light on Tsz-Nephilimus Sapiens culture, religious preferences, and some of their own forefathers.

# SECTION II

# BIBLICAL & LEVANTINE ARCHAEOLOGY

# CHAPTER 7: FACTS & TRUTHS

Biblical archaeology is the scientific study of past lands, cultures, artifacts, events, and people associated with the Bible. Referred to occasionally as Palestinology, Biblical archaeology deals primarily with the Biblical world by way of the Holy Land, although surrounding areas of the Middle East can be included for Biblical archaeology. Like many fields of science, Biblical archaeology can be applied to other areas of archaeological research such as Near Eastern Archaeology, Levantine archaeology, Assyrianology, and Egyptology.

With the application of field research, areas around Israel can yield a treasure trove of information of the past that deals with subjects of agriculture, medicine, ecology, geology, and many modern fields that can benefit Biblical archaeology. The most valuable pieces of information that can be surmised from Biblical archaeology is what can be attained from the studies being conducted on surface areas that while a desert area today, may have been an oasis or fertile area ages before. Modern scientific methods joined with Biblical archaeology are producing amazing discoveries never before realized.

Biblical archaeological records require a thorough examination of the evidence that is presented in the Bible, the Holy Land, and the surrounding areas. Biblical archaeology is a polemic field of study that is the subject of multiple debates and arguments. The importance of Biblical archaeology as a whole is to provide scientific facts and proof of Biblical narratives, artifacts, people, locations, and so forth. There is also a great need to provide historical information of the Jewish ancestry that is being disputed in the world today by such governing bodies of archaeology and political powers such as the United Nations Educational, Scientific, and Cultural Organization (UNESCO), The European Union, and other international governing organizations.

UNESCO has been publicly denouncing the claims of Jewish history in Israel, and has been pushing for more negative positions of favoritism towards the Palestinian and worldviews with questionable, little, or no archaeological backing. Israeli Prime Minister Benjamin Nethanyahu said in an interview with the Huffington Post, "The Theatre of the absurd at UNESCO continues and today the organization adopted another delusional decision which says that the people of Israel have no connection to the Temple Mount and the Western Wall." An application of the scholarly field of Biblical archaeology is important to providing the world with the proof of the Jewish claims in Israel. Biblical Studies is also important to the field of Biblical archaeology for better aid to Biblical interpretation and identification.

Biblical history and prehistory require examination of the Biblical narratives and accounts spread throughout the centuries by Jewish, Christian, and secular scholars and historians. Of particular importance is the need to apply the written accounts of the Bible with field research done by field archaeologists digging and searching for the historical evidence of the Bible left behind in the grounds of where character figures and peoples of the Bible once walked, lived, and thrived. Biblical archaeology uses most of the same methods of scientific techniques that general fields of archaeology use, with one notable exception of attention to evidence and theories taken from the Bible. Similar application of narrative research was done by businessman and archaeologist Heinreich Schliemann in his search for the city of Troy in Turkey in 1870 from accounts in Homer's books *The Iliad* and *The Odyssey*.

One of the most important methodologies for further growth in Biblical archaeology is to connect the chronological accounts from the Bible to the timelines of other civilizations. A timeline of the rise of the various religions, cults, rituals, and sacred sites from Paleolithic, Neolithic, Copper, and Bronze Age roots would further aid the vital connecting points of the histories and civilizations of the Bible. The real first timeline begins with the study of the first periods of Biblical history, or pre-history.

Periods and timelines in Biblical archaeology predominantly begin around the Neolithic timeline of 8500 BC (Before Christ). Paleolithic timelines should be included in Biblical timelines for historical connections to various cultures that can be applied to later time periods. Being polemical (multiple arguments) allows Biblical archaeology to have a wide range of standards and practices for use in the science of uncovering archaeological secrets. It is important to apply the Bible to a specific timeline that coincides with other historical chronologies. The reason for such an application is to help further trace the roots of various people that have occupied the Holy Land, to establish the authenticity claims to the land via heritage sites such as the Jewish people of Israel (a very heated topic the world over today) and the ethnic Chaldeans and Assyrians of Syria and Iraq, as well as to other groups who have established an unrecognized homeland, yet have a presence in the region via their ancient roots such as the Kurdish people and their ties to the ancient Medes. The identification of the Jewish roots in Israel would begin with the understanding of their Semitic heritage.

The word *Semitic* refers commonly to Semitic language groups. The word Semitic in today's world refers to Jewish people of religious and national identification. The word Semitic more accurately refers to several ancient groups. Those ancient groups include Nomads, Bedouins, Ethiopians such as those from Harari and Tigrayans, Assyrians, Amorites, and Samaritans. Many Semitic ancestors can be traced back passed Abraham all the way to Shem who fathered the Semite peoples.

The roots of Semitic people that would become part of the modern world like the Israelis, Arabs, and other Middle Eastern ethnicities and minorities such as Kurds and Druze of Syria, Lebanon, and Israel originate in the lands once called Mesopotamia. Other groups such as Palestinians and Turks would migrate to the Middle East (mostly from regions of Russia) over the course of history following the collapse of the Eastern part of the Roman Empire called the Byzantine Empire. Many Semitic tribes existed in the cradle of Civilization called Mesopotamia during the Bronze Age. Much of their roots go back to older groups of the Neolithic Age.

The Neolithic Age (old stone) was the beginning of the societies that would give rise to civilizations that would turn into future people and kingdoms of the Bible. Without the contributions of many of the cultures that migrated into the Levant, the Fertile Crescent, and other areas, then the history of the Bible may have been quite different. The presence of foreign influences in the lands from the east toward Africa and Europe played a heavy part in the cultivation of the future civilizations that would rise to create the cradle of civilization called Mesopotamia.

It is from Mesopotamia that the very first true civilizations began at approximately 3500 BC during the Bronze Age. According to Biblical and Levantine archaeology, the Bronze Age falls under the three-age system of chronology for the dating of time periods, artifacts and events of late prehistory, and early history. The three-age system of chronology timeline is the Stone Age (pre-history to 3300 BC), Bronze Age (3300 BC to 1200 BC), and Iron Age (1200 BC to 500 BC).

The early history of the Middle East is based on two areas of importance. The first is domestic inhabitants, and the second is migrants who came to the Middle East. Predominately, the migrants were the main inspiration for practices that would be adapted by domestic and future migrants that would adapt to their new homeland for the next several thousand years. Migrants from the east were the first people to introduce new techniques for building, foraging, agriculture, and other important traits that would be accepted, adopted, and later integrated into the civilizations that would later arise in the Copper and Bronze Ages.

Many places throughout the world from Africa to Europe established 'societies' that would turn into kingdoms and civilizations. Mesopotamia however is considered the first actual civilization due to their development rate and influence other cultures took from the examples of Mesopotamian culture. Society and civilization differs as societies become civilizations, but civilizations don't become societies.

A society is defined as a group of people involved in persistent social interaction, and as a social grouping of people in the same geographical territory normally subject to the same political authority, dominant expectations, and cultural expectations. A civilization is defined as any complex society that is characterized by urban development, social stratification, symbolic communication forms such as language and writing, and separation and dominion over the natural environment by the cultural elite. In a more broad sense, a society evolves into a civilization through a series of specific circumstances and events.

Many societies come before the three-age system during time-periods called the Chalcolithic and Neolithic periods. The Neolithic period (New Stone Age) deals with the development of human technology at around 8500 BC, to 4300 BC. The Chalcolithic (Copper Age) is the beginning of human technology involving the use of metal alloys. The Chalcolithic period ranged from 4300 BC to 3300 BC. Following the Chalcolithic period or Copper Age would come the Bronze Age. The Bronze Age is when the Mesopotamian civilization would arise around 3500 BC.

From Mesopotamia, civilization in its more finely tuned essence, sprang forth hence its identification as the cradle of civilization. Mesopotamia is a Greek word meaning the land between two rivers. Those two rivers are the Tigris and Euphrates. Mesopotamia was a large and vast territory covering such modern day countries as (but not limited to) Kuwait, Iraq, and Iran. Each modern nation that made up territory of Mesopotamia played an integral part in the growth and development of the economic, agricultural, and seafaring powers of Mesopotamia and future empires and kingdoms that would come to the future ages.

Biblical narratives usually contain more details than often noticed upon first glance. Biblical descriptions from narrations of religions and cults are a subject of particular interest. Throughout the Middle East are countless sites that have yet to be fully explored. All civilizations have origins that date back to a progenitor meaning something from which others are descended or originate.

Most of the early inhabitants of the Middle East settled in mountainous regions. The purpose of living in such areas was for the use of caves for shelter, big-game animals, fresh spring water, and observation of certain spiritual practices. Taking directions from Genesis 2:8 and 11:2 about people coming from the east (or eastward), many of the early people of the earth came from the west in Africa to the east in Asia.

The earliest human remains of Homo Sapien bones estimated to be around 195,000 years old were found in the Kibish Mountains of Ethiopia. The discovery of those human remains would place their timeline existence at the Middle Paleolithic Era. The second earliest site of modern human remains was discovered at Herto Bouri, Ethiopia. The human remains from Herto Bouri are dated to be from 155,000-160,000 BC. The Kibish Mountains discovery helps shed light on why man was moving eastward to Asia. The migration, according to theory, was in order to collect cave minerals for stone tool making known as speleothem, which was becoming nonexistent due to dry weather in the caverns of the Levantine land bridge that migrants crossed to reach Asia. That meant Stone-Age man was moving from Africa to Asia to procure more abundant resources in areas with more caves and mountain resources. Early man was more defined by simpler terms of living, and perhaps was one reason man would move eastward towards the area that the Bible refers to as Eden (the garden of Eden was described as 'in Eden') was a paradise with an abundance of food, water, animals, and shelter.

Prehistoric societies were more primitive in terms of skills for developing technological based cultures. Only in the course of humanity developing agriculture as a means of life for food and clothing did social orders called hunter-gatherers develop further into agriculture based social orders. The development of agricultural societies from hunter-gatherers would produce more complicated societies, and from the rise of those more complex cultures would come the production of evolved religious systems similar to theocracy based hierarchies. Prehistoric man practiced spirituality, but their practices were more philosophical based thinking, as opposed to organized religious style belief (what is man, who is God, etc.).

Hierarchy based societies would produce priestly systems that would establish high priests as the messengers of the deities that were worshipped by the common people. Religious themed leaders such as shamans, astrologers, magicians, and wise men who would become the advisors to leadership would be established. Many early Biblical groups developed from such beginnings to become some of the most revered civilizations throughout history like Assyrian and Babylonian.

Mountain dwellers are found all over the ancient Middle East. Recent discoveries made around Mt. Ebal by Biblical archaeologist Adam Zertal have uncovered sacred shrines that are believed to be cult sites made from unhewn stones believed to be *Bamah* meaning cultic site or high place. Such examples of cult or sacred sites are discovered at mountain sites where prehistoric groups used caves, open areas, and the natural elements to build shrines and temples for multiple purposes of worship and ritual use.

Biblical archaeologist Adam Zertal excavated several unique pieces of cult artifacts and shrines on Mt. Ebal. Zertal says, "When the Mount Ebal site is set on the larger stage of the Israelite settlement, its origin is seen to be consistent with the dramatic settlement activity in the central hill country during the transition from the Late Bronze to the Iron Age I ("I" represents first part of the Iron Age)." Looking at Iron Age mountain sites in conjunction with older mountain sites outlines a pattern of growth from Stone Age to Iron Age cults.

Biblical and non-Biblical fields of study often differ on timelines and facts. The shared belief that man first originated in Africa and then migrated to Asia and settled in the exact area that Eden is theorized to have existed further adds validation to the scriptures by way of literal mapping and archaeological theory. The development of hunter-gatherer structural societies could have originated with a migration theory of a land bridge that had a limited window of opening to the east of the African belt that would allow them to cross into Asia was a risk early man felt needed to be taken to reach an area more livable and hospitable. To understand the land, the animals, the environment on the way to Asia would be of great value to the species made in God's image who took dominion of the earth, the plants, and animals of the field that Genesis 1:26 and 1:28 explains.

It is vital to see the Bible does not merely occupy the area that makes up ancient Israel and Judah. The lands and history of the Bible span three continents respectively. Ancient human remains are discovered all over Africa, Asia, and Europe. When those humans are examined with scientific methods of mapping their migrations, then a common theme can be found to pinpoint their origins that can connect Biblical locations for the beginnings of humanity and all his species that sprang from the dust of the earth.

# CHAPTER 8: THE EARLY DAYS

The land and sea were meant to be dominated by mankind just as animals were when God appointed man as master of the earth. The earth is filled with the invisible presence of God that is listed in Romans 1:20. Being that there is an invisible presence of God in creation brings into account another side of the spiritual connection to man and the land. A few of the modern nations that made up Mesopotamia such as Kuwait, Iraq, and Iran are some of the earliest examples of economic growth in agriculture, fishing, and sea trade. With those industrial procurement advancements would come advanced spiritual practices that would become polytheistic in nature.

Kuwait was the main area during the Ubaid period in 6500 BC for in-between interactions of Mesopotamia with Eastern Arabia, known today as Bahrain. Mesopotamians and Sumerians first settled Kuwait in 2000 BC. Sumerians from Ur settled on Kuwait's Failaka Island, turning it into a mercantile trading center. The Neolithic inhabitants of Kuwait were among the earliest maritime traders of the world. The ships of the early traders reached China by the 8th Century AD. China and Mesopotamia were one of four areas to have civilizations in the early and late Bronze Age along side Egypt and the Indus Valley.

Egypt is an example of a culture advancing from rural cult practices into a sophisticated religious based society. Egypt practiced a belief system known as Animism. Animism means the attribution of a soul to such things as natural phenomena, plants, and inanimate things. Egypt took the practice of animism and mixed it into a practice of belief that fit into a more civilized age. Pre-Egyptian culture before the first dynasty (3100 BC) is of particular interest due to many customs that were practiced being adopted by the first dynasty. The first dynasty of Egypt appeared during the first part of the Bronze Age called the Early Bronze Age or EB from 3300 to 3050 BC.

Ancient Egypt was notorious for the variety of cults that appeared in their history. The most important cults centered on death. The word cult is defined as a system of religious veneration and devotion directed toward a particular object or figure. Cult is also defined as a small group having religious beliefs or practices regarded by others as strange or sinister, and as a misplaced or excessive administration for a particular person or thing. Egypt practiced all forms of the definitions of a cult.

Ancient Egypt is perhaps the most recognized civilization in history. The Egyptians were known for making the first piece of paper called papyrus. Egyptians practiced mummification with very specific scientific precision for proper burial. Great treaties made between Egypt and foreign powers were inspirations to future generations. One such example of a famous Egyptian treaty is a copy of the treaty between the Egyptians and the Hittites on display at the United Nations headquarters outside the entrance to the Security Council in New York City, New York.

There is considerable evidence to suggest that Ancient Egypt took great influence from the Near East in Asia. Egypt was known to be prejudiced towards anyone and anything not Egyptian or housed within the borders of Egypt. Egyptians did not like leaving their own country unless it was for trade, conquest, or diplomatic reasons. The first pre-dynastic leaders of Egypt perhaps had more dealings with foreigners than later dynasties, but it is known that Egypt has had at least three dynasties from the 13th to 15th that were of Canaanite origin called the Hyskos. While rulers of a later period, the end result of the Hyskos presence in Egypt is that Egypt did have a steady cultural exchange with foreigners throughout their history.

Following the tenth dynasty is when more prejudiced views by Egyptians happened due to the amount of migrants into the country including the foreign rulers of the Hyksos who were in charge of Lower Egypt, which occurred from the 13th to the 15th dynasty. Though the Hyksos came from Canaan, there are strong chances that they took much of their culture from Mesopotamia and other cultures as Canaan was between Egypt and Mesopotamia. The most frequent of cultures that traded with Egypt and Canaan would come from territories located in modern day Iraq.

Iraq is identified with Mesopotamia, Sumer, Babylon, and other ancient kingdoms of the region. Iraq prehistory is important in consideration of the rise of the future kingdoms and empires. Iraq was once a Neanderthal hub in 65,000 and 35,000 BC. The Shanidar Cave in the Erbil Governate of Iraqi Kurdistan in the Zagros Mountains is home to a Neanderthal archaeological site. Neolithic cemeteries are also present in the same region, an important point of interest as it shows Neanderthals had burial practices, dated to about 11,000 BC of the Neolithic Age. The presence of Neanderthals and later civilizations from the Ubaid period all the way up to the first kingdoms show that Iraq truly was the cradle of civilization. Aside from its cultural contributions, Iraq was made famous for its historical developments in agriculture and cattle raising.

Beginning in 10,000 BC, Iraq was growing in agriculture and cattle breeding alongside Asia Minor and the Levant. Agriculture, tool making, and architecture were making major advancements between 6500 and 3800 BC of the Ubaid period. The development of agriculture grew further in the regions of Iran. Iran developed agricultural breakthroughs around the tenth to the eighth millennium BC around the Zagros region. Iran also has famous Neanderthal archaeological sites similar to those found in Iraq. Neanderthal sites, like in Iran are found around the Warwasi rock shelter in Kermanshah, and Yalteh Cave in the Zagros Mountains. The significance of mountains sites and cave sites is prevalent with the rise of the agricultural and maritime breakthroughs for reasons of religious and cult beliefs that would influence the entire region over time.

Agriculture, cattle raising, hunting, and even fishing would help influence the rise of polytheism and pantheism in the religions of the world. Polytheism is defined as the belief or worship of more than one god. Pantheism is the tolerance and worship of all gods. Pantheism is also defined as a belief or doctrine identifying God with the universe, or the universe as a manifestation of God.

The whole world has religions based in pantheistic beliefs. Belief in a single god or one god is known as Monotheism. In the modern world, Christianity, Judaism, and Islam are the three main religions that practice monotheism.

Such practices would develop from the earlier religious and spiritual concepts of Animism and Shamanism that would seek to identify spirits in both living and non living things, and the belief that a person could speak on behalf of those spirits or gods, or be possessed by them. Mesopotamia was famous for its multiple gods and goddesses that represented a double or triple authority nature over such things as seasons, harvests, fishing, fertility, hunting, herding, and other areas societies turned to the gods for in order to gain a positive outcome.

Mesopotamia and surrounding territories helped to introduce the world to the civilized religious age. The Mesopotamians established one of the first religious based civilizations in the fourth millennium. The religious beliefs of Mesopotamia revolve primarily around Sumer, Assyria, Akkad, and Babylonia.

The religious beliefs of Mesopotamia is argued to not be influenced by the various peoples that moved in and out of the area, but instead based on tradition and adaption to a syncretic (blending of various practices) style of religious growth up until the end of Mesopotamian civilization. However, there is a common theme of nature worship most undoubtedly influenced by the more primal based early cultures of Mesopotamia as many of the more powerful gods of Mesopotamia and Sumer were derived from being in charge of the weather, the stars, the land, and the sea. Such beliefs were the main beliefs of the hunter-gatherer groups that occupied pre-Mesopotamia and Sumer as only when the weather and seasons were good could animals be more abundant to hunt, and the land could produce more to eat and make clothing and other everyday living materials.

*Assyrian Lion Hunt Courtesy of Ricardo Tulio Gandelman*

Biblical scripture warns of spiritual practices pertaining to the worship of stars and nature. Deuteronomy 4:19 ESV says, *"And beware lest you raise your eyes to heaven, and when you see the sun and the moon and the stars, all the host of heaven, you be drawn away and bow down to them and the Lord your God has allotted to all the peoples under the whole heaven."*

The main components of deity worship in ancient Mesopotamia were based around particular gods and goddesses who had dual representations as solar deities representing the sun, moon, and the stars, plus everyday activities such as farming, bartering, building, and ruling. The most important of the god ruling authorities were those that controlled nature.

Mesopotamia was not a rich country as it progressed ecologically. Building materials were imported as products like clay and shale for brick making, and timber for lumber were scarce. Rivers would often flood and damage fertile areas that farming and cattle raising was conducted. Even wildlife could be treacherous, as predators such as lions could become a pestilence to people. One account of lions becoming a major burden on an entire people is witnessed in 2 Kings 17:25 when God sent lions among the Assyrians for their sins, and is accounted by the Assyrians in murals of kings hunting lions by chariot or killing them bare handed.

The underlying reasons that civilizations rise was due to the advancement of cities, and the development of cities would lead to writing and records. With the rise of writing and records came the beginnings of history. History is built not only on facts and true accounts, but also on stories, songs, poems, and art that depict great deeds that inspire reasons to learn and preserve them. Without tales that inspire people to learn and build on great deeds, heroes, and events of history that were told in a way that brought a sense of wonder and desire to follow, pursue, and try to relive, then history would not be as important to a civilization as other areas of pursuit. Religion would not be as important were it not for the same reasons history is often portrayed.

Many histories begin with creation stories. Other histories deal with heroes, nature, breakthroughs for science, and spiritual stories that open the human mind to seek more understanding of the unknown. In the civilizations of Biblical archaeology, hunting is one area that history is built upon as it involves in one example struggle between life and death. Some of the earliest kings and tribal chiefs of the Bible were hunters in the very beginning.

# CHAPTER 9: HUNTERS & SACRED RITES

Much of the cultural facts known about Mesopotamia usually revolve around the worship of nature and the cosmos. However, like ancient Egyptian gods, Mesopotamian kingdoms had gods that represented multiple positions besides stars and nature. Some gods represented seasons and stars, some harvest and fertility, hunting and war, and life and death.

Temples and cities were built in particular areas to represent a particular cult of a god that was centered in a specific location for reasons of alignment under a particular constellation at a certain time of year, a special event that happened on a site that made the area sacred, the site was considered a good location for strategic reasons, or it was rich land for economical benefits and therefore appropriate for settlements to be developed. Many hunter-gatherers settled in particular areas for such reasons with the exception that they often merged all the reasons together and would center their culture on community practices.

The connecting factors between the hunter-gatherers of Mesopotamia, and the societies that formed over time from the Neolithic Age into the Bronze Age were the first rulers and their systems of government. It is very likely the first rulers aside from tribal chiefs were hunter-gatherers that gradually became more civil after moving away from rural practices and into more city style societies. The first ruler of the land of what would become Mesopotamia is named Nimrod.

Nimrod is listed in Genesis 10:8-112 KJV:

*"And Cush begat Nimrod: he began to be a mighty one in the earth. He was a mighty hunter before the Lord: wherefore it is said, Even as Nimrod the mighty hunter before the Lord. And the beginning of his kingdom was Babel, and Erech, and Accad, and Calneh, in the land of Shinar. Out of that land went forth Asshur, and builded Ninevah, and the city Rehoboth, and Calah, and Resen between Ninevah and Calah: the same is a great city."*

Nimrod is the first king of Shinar or Mesopotamia. His official title when addressed as king was Bel (Master) Nimrod. The mention of the word Bel is found in Jeremiah 50:2, after the proclamation of Babylon being taken (captured) by future enemies. Jeremiah 50:2 in the King James Translation says, *"Declare ye among the nations, and publish, and set up a standard; publish, and conceal not: say, Babylon is taken, Bel is confounded, Merodach is broken in pieces; her idols are confounded, her images are broken in pieces."* Bel is an ancient Babylonian word for lord or master usually identified with various gods of Babylonia.

Many scholars have surmised that Bel Nimrod was the king who built the tower of Babel due to his first kingdom being Babel. Bel Nimrod possibly gained his status as a ruler from his merits as a hunter and possibly a tribal chief that eventually turned into a kingship. Hunters are important figures in many societies, especially in Mesopotamia and Assyria.

In the ancient world hunters were often the heroes of stories such as the Egyptian goddesses of hunting called Neith, Wepwawet, and Pakhet, or the Hittite god of hunting, Rundas. Hunting gods can be more influential on history than other ancient world deities due to their exciting hunting stories. In Sumerian and Babylonian literature, the king of Ur Gilgamesh and the wild forest man Enkidu hunted and killed the Bull of Heaven that terrorized many people. Such figures inspired royalty and military to adopt certain customs such as in Assyria where a king had to complete a special lion hunt in order to be accepted by their gods as the true king.

Many nations in the world today use symbols associated with ancient hunting gods. The Hittite god Rundas was expressed with a hunting symbol of a twin headed eagle with rabbits in each talon. The Rundas symbol was adopted by the Roman Empire to represent the western and eastern empires with one eagle head that faced west, and the other head facing east. The twin headed eagle is still used in the world today by many Eastern European countries such as Russia, Serbia, Albania, and Montenegro.

Hunters provide food, shelter, and clothing for the family and the community. Hunters can kill big game and vicious prey that are a threat to a society. Hunters can collect trophies such as pelts, heads, or other parts of an animal that is considered worthy of the kill or hunt. Certain kinds trophies can lead to prestige or recognition such as rites of passage into manhood or leadership roles of an individual and acceptance. Hunters can inspire others or be icons for young people to look up to and become hunters, warriors, or soldiers like those who inspired them. Such inspiration can be expressed through stories, songs, and eyewitness accounts of exploits that were extraordinary.

Standard kings like other kingdoms did not rule the people

of Sumer, Babylon, and Akkadia. The kings of the kingdoms of Sumer, Babylon, and Akkadia were not born of a bloodline of royalty in the normal sense like other kingdoms. In the early days of Babylon, Akkadia, and Sumer, the king or city-

king of a city-state was usually a priest or medicine man. Such kings or priests were scholars, healers, scientists, and men of the gods. Bel Nimrod was possibly identified as such a figure of leadership as a king and holy man. Bel Nimrod possibly set the standards for Sumerian, Akkadian, and Babylonian rulers from him as the first king of four kingdoms. Being the first king of Shinar, Bel Nimrod is or was considered to be similar or the same as Zoraster, the prophet and founder of the religion called Zorastrianism.

Being given the label "a mighty hunter before the Lord" would give Bel Nimrod a unique title with an almost *anointed* quality. The word *before* is of great importance to the description of Bel Nimrod. The word before can have several meanings. The word *before* can have a literal meaning of 'that which turns.' The word can also have a figurative meaning such as to refer to meaning a direction of facing, before, in front of, or against. It is the last definition of "against" that Nimrod is associated with, as he is believed to have been *against* God.

Bel Nimrod was an individual that was among the first after the flood to induce worship and adoration not to God, but to other things. There are many ideas that speculate why Bel Nimrod would not worship God. Some reasons Bel Nimrod was against God fall under three theories:

1. The kingdoms that Bel Nimrod founded did not reverence God or practice monotheistic (worship of one god) worship, but instead observed polytheistic (worship of multiple gods) religions and worship.

2. The kingdoms of Mesopotamia often maintained a "worthy of self" mentality that was seen with many of the kings of the various empires. Bel Nimrod is considered to be the king who undertook the building of the city and tower of Babel, which is seen as a symbol of mankind glorifying people instead of God and leading to pride and arrogance. Bel Nimrod's hunting attributes could add to his fame and rise to power.

3. According to Genesis 11:6, the people who came from the east and dwelt in Shinar were one language, one voice, and nothing they did would be impossible. It is likely the people were committing evil acts that were against God, thus leading to the mixing of languages and the scattering of the people of Shinar to other parts of the earth.

Modern American tales of inspiration and legendary exploits deal greatly with stories and tales of hunting and survival. Hunters and outdoorsmen such as Daniel Boone, Davy Crockett, Theodore Roosevelt, and Ernest Hemmingway were some of the men that aspired to greatness from their hunting exploits. Those same men became congressmen, presidents, and great authors. It is not hard to apply the same ideas of legends and exploits that would lead hunters to positions of power in the modern age to the rulers of ancient world. Tales of glory, heroic exploits, and great hunts can lead men and women to positions of authority in any age.

Following the word *before*, the next word *mighty* is another important link to Bel Nimrod. The word *mighty* is used in Genesis 6 to another group of people. Genesis 6:1-4 KJV reads:

*"And it came to pass, when men began to multiply on the face of the earth, and daughters were born unto them, that the sons of God saw the daughters of men that they were fair, and they took wives for themselves all of which they chose. And the Lord said, My Spirit shall not always strive with man, for that he also is flesh: yet his days shall be an hundred and twenty years. There were giants in the earth in those days; and also after that, when the sons of God came in unto the daughters of men, and they bare children to them, the same became mighty men which were of old, men of renown."*

The phrase "mighty men" could be where Bel Nimrod's identification as a "mighty one" and a "mighty hunter" could derive.

Mighty is defined as possessing great power or strength, with special emphasis on occasion with attention to size. Whether Bel Nimrod was a giant in the literal or figurative sense is not known. If he was associated with the Genesis 6 giants is what is relevant. While it is worthwhile to discover if giants of the Bible did exist or not, the focus on Nimrod and the Genesis 6 mighty men is not based on actual size accounts. What is important of note with Nimrod is considered his status as a mighty man in association with the men of renown.

Kings often will identify themselves with feats of might to

set themselves up as absolute authority figures. Bel Nimrod would undoubtedly achieve a position of master or ruler using the same tactics. The four kingdoms that he would establish are one way to show testament to his level of authority.

As previously mentioned, kings of Mesopotamia and Sumer were holy men, and Assyrian kings participated in religious hunts to kill lions in order to be accepted as true kings by the gods. Bel Nimrod is perhaps the first king to practice such customs. Bel Nimrod's estimated kingship is about the late early Bronze Age, but that is debatable. Several ruins of Mesopotamia are named after Nimrod by $8^{th}$ century Arabs. The kingdoms of Bel Nimrod when identified with their non-biblical counterpart kingdom names are as follows:

1. **Accad-Babylonian Akkad, capital of the Akkadian Empire.**

2. **Babel-Hebrew Bible name for Babylon, capital of the Neo-Babylonian Empire and what South Mesopotamia would later be known as due to Babylon growing in size.**

3. **Calneb- believed to be Nippur, one of the most ancient cities of Sumer and special site of worship to the Sumerian god Enlil.**

4. **Erech-Uruk, largest city in the world during the $4^{th}$ century, and royal seat to the legendary King Gilgamesh.**

All of these cities would become key city-states and capitals of later empires.

Bel Nimrod ruled over all four of these cities and the nation of Shinar or Mesopotamia that he established, but Bel Nimrod has much more to offer as a ruler besides the foundation of some of the most important archaeological sites in the modern world. Bel Nimrod would most likely be a hunter-gatherer type figure that developed from a tribal society chief into a civilized king of early Shinar or Mesopotamia. It can be surmised that Bel Nimrod practiced spiritual beliefs that reflected his chosen profession as a hunter.

Bel Nimrod was possibly born and raised a hunter-gatherer. A hunter-gatherer is a person living in a society that thrives off of the collection of wild plants and the pursuing or hunting of wild animals. Such pursuit of plants and animals in terms of survival is known as foraging. Foraging incorporates hunting into the lifestyle of both solitary foraging and group foraging.

Bel Nimrod perhaps was an expert in foraging by way of strategy, use of tools, and decision-making. Bel Nimrod could have possibly developed the ingenuity to develop his kingdoms by being an expert in what is called *decision theory*. Decision theory is the study of the reasoning underlying an agent's (decision makers) choices that include normative (best decision making) theory, and descriptive (irrational decision making) theory. The application of decision theory to Bel Nimrod could be an asset in growing from a hunter into one who "began to be a mighty one" on the earth.

The rise of Nimrod from hunter to king as Bel Nimrod is the possible result of two developments. The first is the development from foraging to agricultural driven expansion of large territories such as the Fertile Crescent and the need for the development of cities with functioning governments to expand growing populations. That would make sense, as the foundation of four kingdoms would have hundreds to thousands of citizens with a great demand for food and shelter. Agriculture and cattle raising would contribute to the development from tribe to kingdom status. The second development is the blending of a government with religion to form a theocracy (a government in which a deity is the source of all authority) based kingdom.

Bel Nimrod and his people most likely practiced what is called Animism and Shamanism. Animism and shamanism are considered the oldest known belief systems (possibly religions) in the world. The definition of animism was developed in the social science of anthropology. Sir Edward Tylor made the current accepted definition of animism in anthropology in the late 19th century. Sir Edward said in regards to animism and anthropology that the definition of animism is, "one of anthropology's earliest concepts, if not the first."

The difference between the definition of animism and the origin of the belief involves non-scientific speculation. How it originated is likely outside of the human historical record. How it was defined during its origins is largely lost to humanity. In such regards, the biological evolution of human cognition has much to say about the natural inclination to

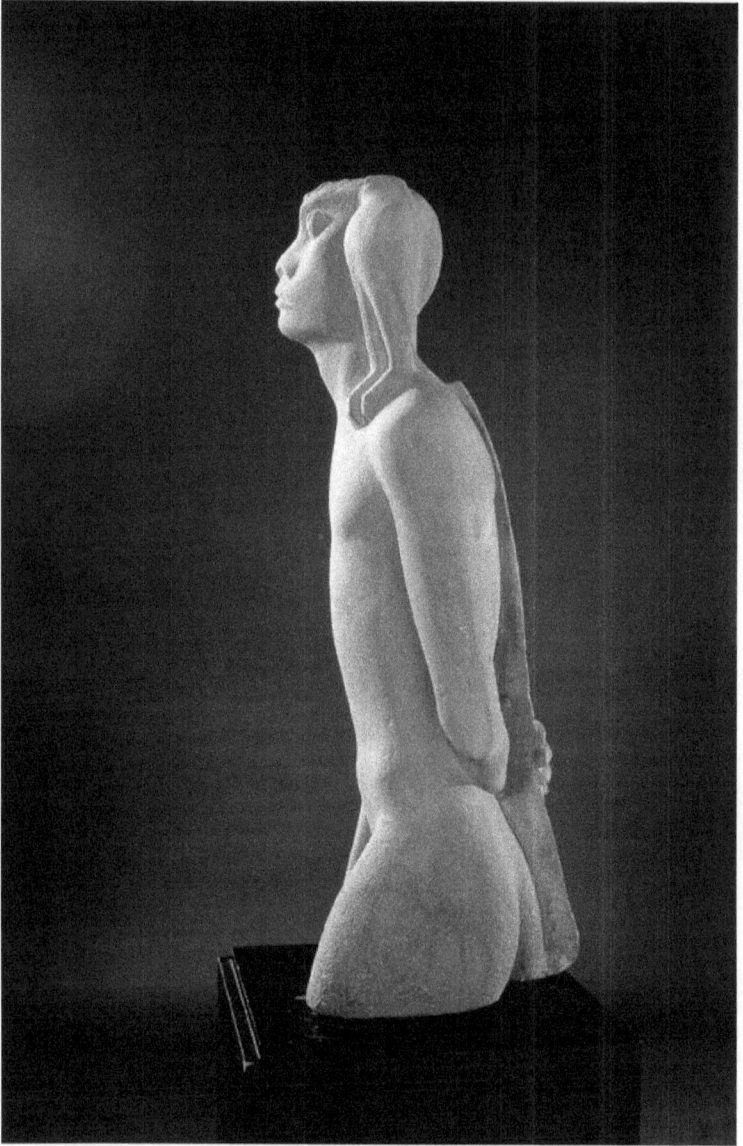

*Sculpture of Nimrod Courtesy of Artist Yitzhak Danziger

grant an agency to things that might not be biological in nature.

The descendants of Tsz-Nephilimus Sapien likely had the same beginnings for religion that other early human species had developed. Those beginnings would include religious leadership, rituals, sacred sites, and symbolism for deities and cultural items that were considered holy to gaze at, hold, or touch. Such beginnings would give rise to *devotion* and the *will* to defend the religious beliefs of the practitioners. A strong willed belief can give rise to the idea that *force* could be an appropriate response in certain situations as force is violence. Violence is a supreme authority that many other authorities derive from in order to exercise will or power over others.

Bel Nimrod could very likely have used his position as a mighty hunter to impose his own force upon those who he subjugated as a ruler of four kingdoms. Acts 24:7 KJV states, *"But the chief captain Lysias came upon us, and with great violence took him away out of our hands."* Violence has often been the main method of force religious minded people have used to forward their own agendas. Zephaniah 3:4 KJV, *"Her prophets are light and treacherous person: her priests have polluted the sanctuary, they have done violence to the law."* The use of force to impose ones will on someone else for their own gains or belief is a practice that has been around since the beginning of time and will most likely continue for quite some time.

# CHAPTER 10: NATURE & WORSHIP

It is a common adaption for any species to see a *will* in the elements around it. A predator as opposed to a physical force of nature is different, but each one can be viewed as a force with its own will and purpose. One can't make up tall-tale stories about important elements of human cultures without at least some aspect of truth being in the details. The things that inspired belief are found in the environment, in nature, and human development and they are what pushes it and give more inspiration to story-telling attributes to further add to stories inspirational abilities. Some particular history may have happened millions of years apart from another history, but those histories may have a connection in the belief system that was adapted or adopted by others over time.

It takes the understanding that God is the spiritual presence in nature to understand such a powerful concept. However, mankind often fails to understand such a simple truth and instead believes that the natural and spiritual world produces other kinds of gods and spirits that are in tune with nature. Animism and Shamanism reveal some of the practices that have been nurtured from a lack of understanding the relationship of God and nature that is similar to God and man being the creation shares traits with the creator. The roots of hunting being considered a holy practice goes back to the time Noah exited the ark following the great deluge. The origins of animal hunting and sacrifice start with Noah and commandments from God during a sacrifice Noah made.

Taking details from the time of Noah following the flood of Genesis 7:10, there are precise instructions and dictations given by God to Noah and his family on the relationships between man and nature. The instructions God gave to Noah in Genesis 8:20-22 and 9:1-10 deal specifically with man and their relationship with nature in terms of the earth, animals, seasons, and other issues such as sacrifices and matters of life and death. The scriptures beginning with Genesis 8:20-22 KJV translation states:

*"And Noah builded an altar unto the Lord; and took every clean beast, and of every clean fowl, and offered burnt offerings on the altar. And the Lord smelled a sweet savour; and the Lord said in His heart, I will not again curse the ground anymore for man's sake; for the imagination of man's heart is evil from his youth; neither will I again smite any more every thing living, as I have done. While the earth remaineth, seedtime and harvest, and cold and heat, and summer and winter, and day and night shall not cease."*

From Genesis 9:1-10 KJV, the scriptures read:

*"And God blessed Noah and his sons and said unto them, be fruitful, and multiply, and replenish the earth. And the fear of you and the dread of you shall be upon every beast of the earth and upon every fowl of the air, upon all that moveth upon the earth, and upon all the fishes of the sea; and into your hand are they delivered. Every moving thing that liveth shall be meat for you; even as the green herb have I given you all things. But flesh with the life thereof, which is the blood thereof, shall ye not eat. And surely your blood of your lives will I require; at the hand of every beast will I require it, and at the hand of man; at the hand of every man's brother will I require the life of man. Whose sheddeth man's blood, by man shall his blood be shed: for in the image of God made He man. And you, be ye fruitful, and multiply; bring forth abundantly in*

*the earth, and multiply therein. And God spake unto Noah, and to his sons with him, saying, And I, behold I establish my covenant with you, and with your seed after you; And with every living creature that is with you, of the fowl, of the cattle, and of every beast of the earth with you; from all that go out of the ark, to every beast of the earth."*

There is a connection to the aforementioned scriptures with the human race in a duality of nature and relationship. A relationship established for mankind and nature with God and His blessings. Then, a second relationship established in terms of curses.  The lineage of one of the sons of Noah, Ham, was a lineage cursed during an encounter with a drunk Noah and his sons in Genesis 9:21-26 KJV:

*"And he (Noah) drank of the wine, and was drunken; and he was uncovered within his tent. And Ham, the father of Canaan, saw the nakedness of his father, and told his two brethren without. And Shem and Japeth took a garment, and laid it upon their shoulders, and went backward, and covered the nakedness of their father; and their faces were backward, and they saw not their father's nakedness. And Noah awoke from his wine, and knew what his younger son had done unto him. And he said, "Cursed be Canaan; a servant of servants shall he be unto his brethren. And he said, blessed be the Lord God of Shem; and Canaan shall be his servant. God shall enlarge Japeth, and he shall dwell in the tents of Shem; and Canaan shall be his servant.""*

Noah placed a curse on his own son's child.  The later descendant's of Canaan would be Nimrod and his kingdoms. There is a split from the three sons of Noah that would lead some to worship God, while others to make their own gods.

The beginnings of religious belief start with spiritual belief. Hunting is considered a form of spiritual practice by most cultures. According to a quote by Vermont hunter Robert F. Smith, "Hunting is an ancient dance as old as life itself, written into the very core of what we are as humans." The condition of killing animals that God instructed to Noah in Genesis 9:1-10 define perfectly Robert F. Smith's quote on hunting being what is written into the very core of humans. A scripture in Leviticus adds further legitimacy to hunting having a side of holiness to it through commandments by God for certain customs done with hunting and catching animals.

Leviticus 17:13 KJV states, *"And whatsoever man there be of the children of Israel, or of the strangers that sojourn among you, which hunteth and catcheth any beast or fowl that may be eaten; he shall even pour out the blood thereof, and cover it with dust."*

God wanted anything hunted or caught to be eaten without the partaking of blood from the beast, fish, or bird. Perhaps it was because the blood of an animal was to be used for purification rituals such as spreading blood on burnt offerings for atonement of sins and for offerings of peace such as those outlined in 2 Kings 16:13.

The specifics God used in describing the killing and eating of animals by mankind, and the removal of animal blood presents a godly and spiritual side to hunting similar to how the laws and commandments God gave the Israelites by divine instruction. The essence of killing another life for the need of survival by others is a spiritual practice that God gave specific instructions on when He spoke of it to Noah. The act of taking life for survival is a heavy weight of responsibility and accountability that carries a strong sense of responsibility with it.

It is likely hunting played a major part in the growth from hunter-gatherer societies into early city-states. Originating a practice of searching for food, hunting evolved into a more refined survival art, and later sporting profession. In a study of paleoanthropology, there is a hunting hypothesis that humans evolved more effectively through hunting. There is evidence of stone tools, use of fire, athleticism or more bodily movement for tracking and hunting, and the use of language and religion from a hunting context aided human growth to more sophisticated societies.

Group hunting likely brought about early political structures such as leadership, alliances, and rights of ownership claims over kills from the hunt. Attributes such as courage and power of an individual in a group come from the results of a hunt. Hunting produced prestige among hunters.

In prehistoric times, hunters worshipped deities in the forms of predators and prey. Identifying animals in such a manner is called zoomorphism. Next to zoomorphism is anthropormism. Anthropormorphism is the mixing of human traits with animals. Anthroporophism is associated with the Egyptian pantheon of gods and other supernatural entities such as demi-gods and demons. The Egyptian gods, and deities of other civilizations that practice anthropormorphism used personification or the related attributes of human abstract concepts in their gods such as natural forces like weather, seasons, emotions, and nations themselves. From hunting would arise the need for other markets of growth. Following hunting would be agriculture, and fishing.

Fishing and agriculture play their parts in the development

of eastern civilization. Hunting, while an important factor in building a civilization can only provide so much to a society. Wild game can become scarce to non-existent over time. Fishing and agriculture would then have to become vital assets to survival depending on the availability of the resources needed to produce sufficient amounts of food and supplies to the people of a society or civilization.

Hunting, fishing, and agriculture depend on the state of the land, sea, and air with the right conditions for efficient production of crops, game, and fish. An important field of science that archaeology has taken into use for applying to the study of the ancient world is ecology. Ecology is the scientific study and analysis of interactions among organisms and their environment. Ecology incorporates reactions and conditions of organisms and their environment. Ecology uses biology, geography, and earth science studies. The importance of ecology to Biblical archaeology is the dealings with ecosystems.

The Bible makes several mentions of ecological and environmental events. Ecological and environmental events such as the flood of Noah (Genesis 7), the fourteen years of plenty and famine of Egypt and Canaan (and other areas) during the days of Joseph (Genesis 41), and the three year drought and famine of Elijah (I Kings 17,18) among several others. Each time such natural and supernatural events occurred would not only impact the land of the nation that the ecological disasters occurred in, but also would effect the surrounding areas in small to massive ways. Natural ecological changes would inspire some cultures to develop cults and religions around such phenomenon similar to how star worship would rise from people gazing at the cosmos and considering stars as living gods, deities, other supernatural forces due to the fact that certain stars or constellations would appear at events such as child births, harvest times, weddings, and other events that would be considered coinciding with signs of the heavens. Pseudo and scientific practices such as astrology and astronomy have their roots in those types of basic observations of the cosmos.

Factors to consider are the range, both short and far, the environmental impact on surrounding areas, and the amount of devastation done as an end result. Ecology aids greatly to mapping the ancient lands of the Bible to further the accuracy of understanding Biblical archaeology and history by factoring in the changes such as to terrain and stratigraphy (rock layers).

Turning to fishing and agriculture for food and other factors is the next step in the evolution of a civilization. While animals may become scarce on land, there would be abundant stocks of life in water sources. Depending on the types of soil and seasonal weather in an area, land could be tilled and made to produce food, medicine, clothing, and shelter building with materials such as trees for wood, and binding elements like adhesives. Binding elements can be taken from tar of birch-bark as an example. Another binding element important for building or making other types of adhesives is gum that comes from acacia tree sap that is found all over the Middle East and Africa.

Navigating tens of thousands of years of history reveals much about one culture and their connection to another. Using Biblical accounts for archaeological pursuits also requires a study of the spiritual practices that arise in the peoples of the Bible. Most of the people in the Bible have completely different religious and spiritual practices that range from simple observations and worship of nature that can be seen in hunter-gatherer and early pastoral groups, to more perverse and profane rituals such as human sacrifice and cannibalism that Amorites and Assyrians practiced. Religion like hunting, fishing, and agriculture has a way of evolving from the simple into the more complex.

The spiritual practices of Animism occurred around the time hunter-gatherers were beginning to communicate with each other to begin building up civilizations from Troglodytes (cave dwellers) into city builders. Animism (as mentioned) is the oldest known system of belief in the world. Animism is defined as a religious belief that states various objects, places, and creatures that possess spiritual qualities. Another way of defining animism is that both animate and inanimate things are alive with their own spirit. Many animist religions use animals in their practices. Egyptian gods are associated with animals and human traits. It is possible that the rise of such beliefs stemmed from practices from ancient Turkey and the hunter-gatherers who migrated to various territories of the Middle East. Many ancient hunter-gatherer sites such as Gobekli Tepe in Turkey have shown buildings that are a combination of hunting lodge, meetinghouse, and religious worship sites. Many other such buildings and archaeological excavations are spread all over the Middle East.

Animism is a hunter-gatherer religion and belief system that would grow over time and integrate into the modern world. Many of today's new world religions practice forms of animism. Among the religions of the modern times that practice animism, though those religions will not necessarily

acknowledge such practices having a connection to animism, are Shintoism, Buddhism, Hinduism, Islam, and several folk religions of Asia. Countries that Animism can be seen more expressed in the religious customs of Central and Southeast Asia, Japan, and Taiwan.

The spiritual practices of Animism and other ancient beliefs may have been among the common beliefs of Tsz-Nephilimus Sapiens and their descendants. It has been considered that some tribes of giants did, at one point live in Turkey. Many Greek myths surrounding giants, heroes, and gods are derived from the ancient Greek culture that comes from Turkey, as essentially Turkey and Greece were the "same" culture, at one point. One major theory surrounding the tribes of giants that occupied Canaan and surrounding territories during the days of the Old Testament is that the descendants of Tsz-Nephilimus Sapien (and Tsz-Nephilimus Sapiens themselves) were both stargazers and star worshippers.

Deuteronomy 4:16-19 KJV states, *"Lest ye corrupt yourselves, and make you a graven image, the similitude of any figure, the likeness of male or female, the likeness of any beast that is on the earth, the likeness of any winged fowl that flieth in the air, the likeness of any thing that creepeth on the ground, the likeness of any fish that is in the waters beneath the earth: And lest thou lift thine eyes unto heaven, and when thou seest the sun, and the moon, and the stars, even all the host of heaven, shouldest be driven to worship them, and serve them, which the Lord thy God hath divided unto all nations under the whole of heaven."*

Many sites that have been associated with giant tribes, Neanderthal sites, and other places such as Gobekli Tepe are believed to have been sites used for stargazing and worship. Tsz-Nephilimus Sapiens possibly worshipped the stars of heaven. Gobekli Tepe and other places may be cult sites.

# CHAPTER 11: TROPHY SKULLS & ORACLES

The ancient world evolved their societies into more advanced civilizations while bringing animism into the heart of their many religions. Architecture and art are examples of people taking inspiration from the natural world and building structures and monuments as tribute to those inspirations that would be worshipped or deified. The Bible makes several references to the practice of animism. However, the practice of animism predates Biblical accounts by way of hunter-gatherer groups that arrived long before even the father of Abraham, (Terah) was born. Among the many groups and cultures that inhabited the Middle East in the Stone Age that practiced animism are the Natufians and Ubaidians.

5,000 years before Abraham was born is when the first settlers arrived in what would be called Mesopotamia. The first inhabitants of Mesopotamia were called Ubaidians. The Ubaidians occupied Mesopotamia between 4500 and 4000 BCE (before the common era). They are called proto-Euphrateans who did not speak the Sumerian language. The village of Tell al- Ubaid, located in modern Dhi Qar Province, Iraq, is where the earliest and very large scale excavation of what is called the Ubaid period occurred.

The term Ubaid was created at a conference in Baghdad in 1930 at the same time the Uruk periods were being defined. The excavation of Tell al-'Ubaid was conducted first by English Egyptologist, Henry Hall, and later by archaeologist Charles Woolley. The area is based in an alluvial plain, a flat landform created by deposition of sediment over long periods of time by rivers that come from highland regions forming alluvial soil. One of the more common recurring themes of observation of the location of Mesopotamia is the recurring flooding that occurs in the area annually. The Ubaid period lasted between 6500 and 3800 BCE when the Uruk period took its place. However, there exists two Ubaid periods of two different timespans as North Mesopotamia had their Ubaid period exist from 5300 to 4300 BCE, while a different Ubaid period arrived 1,200 years later.

The Ubaid period brought with it the earliest possible origins of Mesopotamian and Sumerian religious practices. Many idols and statues have been excavated from the areas that the Ubaidians came together to worship their various gods. In the great civilization of Sumeria are archaeological discoveries at the Al Ubaid archaeological site that show early Ubaid culture that is dated to about 7,000 years ago. Among the artifacts discovered at Al-Ubaid is a series of figurines that are humanoid and reptilian in description.

The Ubaidian culture is a prehistoric culture that settled in Mesopotamia. The exact origins of the Ubadians are unknown just as the Sumerian cultures roots are unknown. The Ubaidians lived in large village settlements of mud-brick houses and their own cultures developed architecture, agriculture, irrigation and farming land. The domestic architecture included large T-shaped houses, open courtyards, paved streets, and food processing equipment. Some of the Ubaid villages began to develop into towns, and temples began to appear as well as monumental buildings. Evidence of those buildings is seen in the main Sumerian civilization sites of Eridu, Ur, and Uruk. According to Sumerian texts outside of Biblical reference, Ur is considered the first city.

The main site of where the first humanoid/reptilian like figurines were found in Al-Ubaid is a small mound of about half a kilometer in diameter, and two meters above ground. Harry Reginald Hal first excavated the site in 1919. Both male and female figurines were discovered in different postures and in most of the figurines were found to hold a staff or scepter that is possibly a symbol of justice and ruling. Each figurine is depicted in a different pose. Female figurines can appear with a suckling child. This is perhaps a fertility type of statue as such figures were a common theme among the idols discovered in Mesopotamia. What the figures represent is not exactly known, though an agriculture or fertility possibility is associated with what the figures may represent.

The lizard/snake-like appearances gives off an animal totem type of feel. A similar type of figurine was found at Hurvat Minhah in Israel, with an elongated head and eyes similar to grain kernels (Mazar 1992, 52). The figurine is considered a mother goddess figure, yet such a claim is still only theoretical. The Hurvat Minah figurine and Mesopotamian figures possibly represent a common theme. In regard to the possible theme of the statues, they could be related to animism.

According to archaeologists, the various statue postures such as the females who are breastfeeding infants don't suggest ritualistic themes. However, archaeologists are unsure of their exact nature and therefore their roles continue to remain unknown. Many of the archaeologists agree that because the statues depict common activities such as infant breast-feeding; the Ubaid male and female statues were stylized versions of flesh and bone creatures.

The ancient Ubaidian culture seemed to care greatly for their statues. Between Sumerian and Ubaidian cultures, the serpent is a major symbol used among the societies to represent a number of gods. Among the Sumerian gods that a snake symbol represented was the god known as Enki. In Sumerian mythology, Enki is the god of creation, intelligence, crafts, and several kinds of water, fertility, magic, and mischief. Although usually represented by a goat, fish, or a hybrid of both animals (also known as a Chimera), Enki was represented at times by a serpent symbol or caduceus. A caduceus is the traditional symbol of the Greek god Hermes (messenger god) and features two snakes winding around a staff or staff adorned with wings. Such countries as the United States of America occasionally use the caduceus by mistake as a symbol for modern medicine that is actually represented by the Rod of Asclepius represented as the Star of Life.

The use of snakes in symbolism is apparent in the many places that the Biblical figure Abraham both visited and settled. Abraham was born in a city called Ur, or Ur of the Chaldees. Another city that is referenced in relationship with Abraham is the city of Haran. Both Ur of the Chaldees and Harran are centers of lunar or moon worship. Mesopotamia is one of the earliest sites for astronomy and astrology. Many of the ancient cities were centered on places of great celestial observation.

The real beginnings of Mesopotamia don't begin in the land between rivers, but in the area now known as the nation

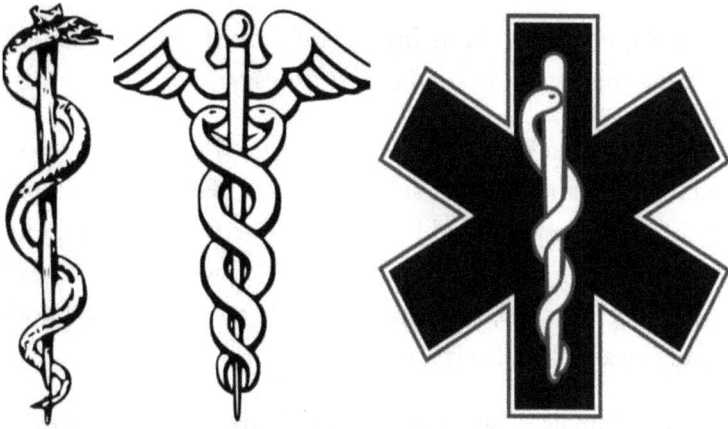

*Rod of Asclepius Courtesy of Hazmat2 (Left), Caduceus Courtesy of Kalki (Middle), Star of Life Courtesy of Verdy P (Middle).*

of Turkey. Before the arrival of the Ubaidians in Mesopotamia, the earliest inhabitants of the Middle East were known as the Natufians. The Natufian settlers existed in 12,000 to 9,500 BCE. Their history trace back to what is known as the Epipaleolithic period. Natufians were a Mesolithic culture. It is possible the Natufians built the first Neolithic settlements of the Levant, a region of the Mediterranean. The Natufian name was made by Dorothy Garrod, who did research in a cave at Wadi an-Natuf, located halfway between Jaffa and Ramallah known as the Shuqba cave.

The Natufians were the earliest agriculturalists. Throughout modern excavations of Israeli and West Bank archaeological sites are traces of the tools and farming plants that were harvested by the Natufians. The Natufians were possibly using methods of agriculture adopted from another group of Levant settlers known as the Kebaran culture. Another possibility is the Natufians used methods learned

121

from Africa either from immigrants, or trade with settlers crossing the Levant into other territories.

Both the Natufians and Ubaidians used the same style of architecture and artistic styles in their respected cultures. Their similar styles would also be viewed in their religious objects. The most common type of religious artifact used as both objects of idol worship and oracle consultation by both cultures was called Teraphim.

Teraphim is a late Latin word derived from the Greek word *theraphin,* and from the original Hebrew word *teraphim.* Teraphim are mentioned in Biblical scriptures of the Old Testament. Teraphim serve two particular purposes. The first is as household gods or idols of ancient Semitic and earlier cultures. The second is they are used for divination practices such as oracles and manifestation objects. Depending on the translation used, teraphim are identified in Biblical scripture either by the name teraphim, as household gods, carved images, oracles, or manifest objects. Scriptures that identify teraphim by name or named for their function are mentioned in several parts of the Bible including in Genesis 31:19,35, Judges 17:5, 18:17, 1 Samuel 19:13, 2 Kings 23:24, Ezekiel 21:21, Hosea 3:4, and Zechariah 10:2.

Teraphim are made into many different types of figures and forms. The most prominent types of teraphim are made in the shapes of humans that include full body types and head shaped idols. Head shaped teraphim often were made with actual human skulls collected from dead bodies of defeated enemies or non-important deceased people.

Teraphim were often carved or molded into designs that

resembled human type figures. On other occasions actual human remains were used in the creation of teraphim. The use of human skulls for teraphim creations was practiced by several groups of the Middle East including Israelites and Amorites. The skulls were often plastered over and decorated to look human. Teraphim of the human skull variety were most commonly used for oracle (predicting of the future) consultations from within the home. The most interesting of teraphim could have been in the possession of the Israelite King David. According to Biblical scriptures of 1 Samuel 19:13,16 KJV, *"And Michal took an image (teraphim), and laid it in the bed, and put a pillow of goats hair for his bolster, and covered it with cloth…And when the messengers were come in, behold, there was an image (teraphim) in the bed with a pillow of goats' hair for his bolster."*

There are several connections to be made with the older Semitic teraphim, and the kingdom of Israel's teraphim to be made from the account of an *image* (teraphim, household god, idol) that was used to impersonate David in his own bed. According to the *New Bible Dictionary*, teraphim "while believed to possibly have come from mummified human heads had no basis in fact." Though this claim was written in 1962, and new archaeological evidence and theories have been made to show teraphim were made of mummified skulls such as teraphim discoveries made in Jericho, there is a unique opportunity to identify the type of teraphim found in the house of David.

In 1 Samuel 17:51, David cut the head of Goliath off after he defeated him at the Valley of Elah. In 1 Samuel 17:54, David brought the head of Goliath to Jerusalem, and placed the armor of Goliath in his own tent. Goliath's sword would go to the high priest Ahimelech at Nob in Jerusalem as read in 1 Samuel 21:9. The significance of the mention of Goliath's head and armor in archeological terms brings to light a possible theme of trophy collecting by King David.

Jewish people in the time of King David were not permitted to worship idols. However, there were other practices that were acceptable among the nation of Israel (and later Judah). One such practice was the keeping of slain enemies heads as teraphim. The word teraphim among Jewish Rabbis described 'disgraceful things.' The keeping of teraphim in a Jewish household was an acceptable act, provided it did not violate Jewish or state law.

For King David, keeping the head of Goliath as a trophy is quite possible as David took the armor and head to Jerusalem, and placed the sword of Goliath in the custody of the priest Ahimelech, which David would later claim as his own sword in 1 Samuel 21:9. For David, the head of the champion of the Philistines to be put on display as a trophy would have brought him great prestige among the military and people of Israel.

The practice itself of the use of teraphim as household gods and plastered skulls preceded the days of Abraham. The city of Jericho contained some of the most preserved plastered skulls in the entirety of Israel when first discovered in 1956. Such examples of teraphim in Jericho and the household of King David are most likely practices adapted from earlier Semitic peoples that adopted their customs from other cultures such as the Natufians.

The Natufian period from 11,000 to 9,000 BC provided an

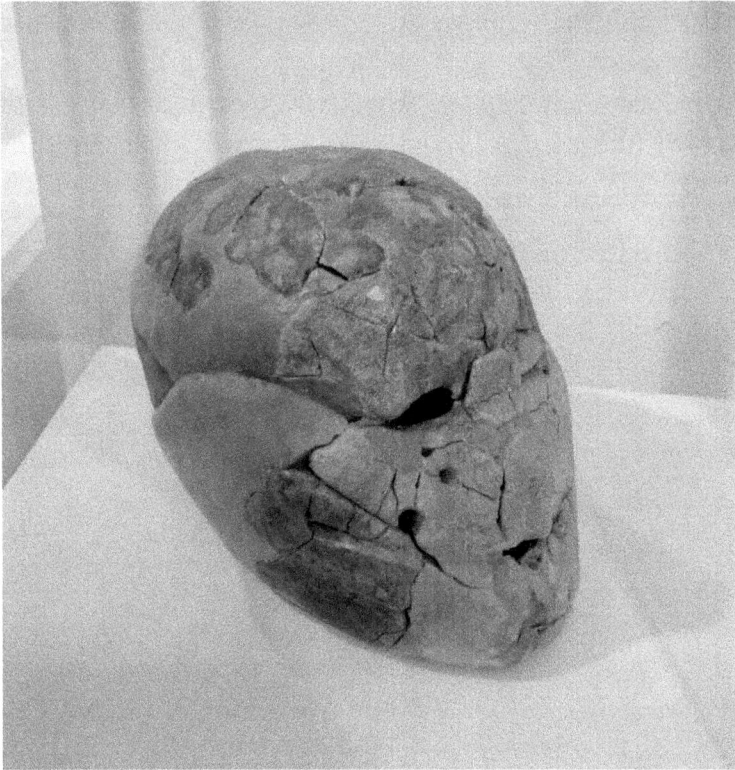

*Beisamoun Plastered Skull, Possible Teraphim Courtesy of Hanay*

example of plastered skulls found in burial sites at Mughararet el-Wad. Many of the skulls were adorned with what appeared to be headdresses and were finely placed in the graves. It is likely that such skulls were teraphim style ornaments that the Natufians used for divination. Natufian culture founded the city of Jericho, perhaps the oldest city in the world. Teraphim plastered skulls were found in abundance in Jericho possibly left by Natufian and later inhabitants.

Teraphim most likely were objects of divination that were

associated with the practice of animism. The book of Deuteronomy lists several scriptures, though not using the term animism, where practices associated with the worship of nature, the cosmos, and images occurred. Deuteronomy 17:2-3 KJV reads:

*"Take ye therefore good heed unto yourselves; for ye saw no manner of similitude on the day that the Lord spake unto you in Horeb out of the midst of the fire: Lest ye corrupt yourselves, and make you a graven image, the similitude of any figure, the likeness of male or female, The likeness of any beast that is on the earth, the likeness of any winged fowl that flieth in the air, the likeness of anything that creepeth on the ground, the likeness of any fish that is in the waters beneath the earth: And lest thou lift up thine eyes unto heaven, and when thou seest the sun, and the moon, and the stars, even all the host of heaven, shouldest be driven to worship them, and serve them, which the Lord thy God hath divided unto all nations under the whole heaven. But the Lord hath taken you, and brought you forth out of the iron furnace, even out of Egypt, to be unto all nations under the whole heaven."*

Next, in Deuteronomy 17:2-3 KJV states, *"And hath gone and served other gods and worshipped them, either the sun, or moon, or any of the host of heaven, which I have not commanded. And it be told thee, and thou have heard of it, and enquired diligently, and behold, it be true, and the thing certain, that such abomination is wrought in Israel."*

It should be noted that God made it clear that no other gods or supernatural things came before Him. God makes Himself evident in Isaiah 43:10 KJV, *"Ye are my witnesses, saith the Lord, and my servant whom I have chosen; that ye may know and believe me, and understand I am He: before Me there was no God formed, neither shall there be after Me."*

The cultic practices of Stone Age groups were the origins of later practices that societies, civilizations, and empires would adopt. They would adapt over time to continue systems of religion that would work until that belief system ultimately would collapse due to it becoming a failed system. Such failed systems would ultimately lead the peoples who practiced them to collapse simultaneously.

Pre-Semitic and non-Semitic inhabitants of Mesopotamia, Canaan, and early Turkish areas were the revolutionary drivers from the Stone Age into the Copper Age, the Bronze Age, and finally the Iron Age. It was the Stone Age roots that made the cultural impact on later societies. Beginning in the last two thousand years of the Epi-Paleolithic period at 10,500 to around 8,500 BC, tribal societies of (mostly) migrants flowed into Canaan and Mesopotamia. Such cultures as the Natufians and Ubaidians were among the most influential hunter-gatherer and agriculture masterminds of the old world. The Natufians and Ubaidians, while separated by different time periods, were perhaps the most important groups of the ancient Middle East.

Natufian culture came before Ubaidian culture by about 3,000 years. Each society lived in two different parts of the Fertile Crescent, yet shared several cultural similarities. They were hunter-gatherers, agriculturalists, and architects of some of the earliest stone and mud-brick buildings. The orthodox conception of primitive cultures into more sophisticated ones is shown through the growth of those two cultures from small to large complex societies.

The importance of Natufian and Ubaidian societies to Biblical archaeology is the adoption of their practices by

*Hall of Prayer for Good Harvests in the Temple of Heaven in Beijing,
China Courtesy of Philip Larson*

future inhabitants in the region. The architecture, art, rituals,
customs, and religions of both cultures would be expanded
as the first kingdoms and empires would arise in 3500 BC.

Natufian and Ubaidian cultures contributed greatly to the
ages that would set the stage for going from the Stone Age to
the Biblical times of the Old and New Testaments. The
overlapping connections that need to be taken into

consideration are the constant intermingling of cultures from Africa and Asia. With the continents so closer together at one point in prehistoric time, the lands of Africa and Asia had more land bridging and other more close connected areas to cross and occupy.

The Tower of Babel itself was built by people possibly from farther into the Orient (the east) than most people previously thought. Genesis 11:2 KJV states, *"And it came to pass, as they journeyed from the east, that they found a plain in the land of Shinar; and they dwelt there."* The phrasing of "journeyed from the east" gives account to the fact that the people who built the Tower of Babel were from farther east than the people who inhabited Shinar. It could be possible that the early people of the kingdoms that would one day make up China created the Tower of Babel.

While the term babel in the Bible has come to mean confusion of languages, the original definition of Babel was the gate of the gods. Many of the Chinese emperors and dynasties built structures, cities, and temples that represented celestial observations and deities fashioned in a similar style to the Tower of Babel as the gate of the gods. One such place would be the Temple of Heaven in Beijing, China. Built in 1406 and completed in 1420, the Temple of Heaven is considered a Taoist temple with the infusion of Heaven Worship (literally the worship of heaven) being incorporated into the temple. Older buildings and temples exist with the same religious and spiritual principles in mind throughout China and surrounding areas.

China, Shinar, and Canaan all have sites that dealt with the worship of stars and heaven. Many sites are said to be sites used by giants and other extinct human species. If such a claim can be backed up with facts, then a rare glimpse can be made of the folk religions and cultic practices of Tsz-Nephilimus Sapiens. Such a discovery would no doubt turn the world of archaeology upside down with new ideas and theories waiting to be explored and proven as real.

# CHAPTER 12: MOUNTAINS & SHRINES

Most sacred places on earth consist of particular locations that coincide with a particular theme. A theme is a subject of talk, writing, thoughts, an exhibition, or a topic of particular interest. Most sacred sites are made holy because the people who made them holy witnessed a miraculous event there, held an event of monumental proportions at the location, or sits on a particular area that has celestial or geographical significance. Such natural occurring events could be a star constellation resting directly over a site once a year, a sacred river once ran over the spot but dried out ages ago, or a battle was fought there and a great victory was won at the site to name some examples that make a particular spot a sacred site. In the ancient world, outdoor locations on mountains and in caves were considered very sacred.

From the late Bronze Age, to the first part of the Iron Age came the discovery of structures on Mt. Ebal in the West Bank that is considered cultic shrines. One example from Mt. Ebal is a six-foot-wide circular depression containing animal bones and ash in the center. Near the depression are remains of chalice, hearths, and remains of ash and animal bones giving the excavators the suggestion the site was a cultic site of some kind for ritual sacrifice.

An altar of unhewn stones was discovered by Adam Zertal at Mt. Ebal that was built over a previous construction. The altar site had no floor or entrance, but was riddled with the bones of male bulls, deer, and Iron Age pottery. Zertal asserted, during an interview in 1985, that such an altar was possibly associated with the altar mentioned in Joshua 8:30-31 KJV, *"Then Joshua built an altar unto the Lord God of Israel in Mount Ebal, as Moses the servant of the Lord commanded the children of Israel, as it is written in the book of the law of Moses, an altar of whole stones, over which no man hath lifted up any iron: and they offered thereon burnt offerings unto the Lord, and sacrificed peace offerings."*

Zertal stated that he believed such a site might have been an early sanctuary for the Israelites. Other critic archaeologists have attempted to disprove Zertal such as Israeli archaeologist Anson Rainey, who called the discovery nothing more than a house, and then called Zertal a "blatant phony." Zertal responded to such accusations by continuing his research of the site on Mt. Ebal. While the results are still controversial among scholars, it is at least generally agreed among scholars that the site is a cult site.

Sites of shrines on mountains are located in several locations throughout Israel and the surrounding territories. Several mountain ranges have produced shrines, sacred caves, and other findings of archaeological intrigue that are considered cult sites. Other mountains of significance next to Mt. Ebal are Mt. Hermon, Mt. Sinai, Mt. Nemrut, Mt. Carmel, and Mt. Horeb along with several others.

Along with mountains and cult shrines come cave sites. Much of the Bible is full of accounts of caves such as the Machpelah cave, where Abraham buried his wife Sarah and later used it as his own burying place as read in Genesis 23:19,20. The Makkedah cave where five kings hid from Joshua in Joshua 10:16. Lastly, the cave that was used as the tomb for Lazarus, before being raised from the dead by Jesus in John 11:38.

Caves are troglodyte dwellings. Troglodyte means people who dwell in caves. The Stone Age produced many cultures that occupied caves, worshipped in caves, buried their dead in caves, and left behind evidence of their culture and heritage in caves. Shamans and witch doctors used caves for cult rituals and religious purposes. Many caves around Mt. Carmel in Israel are home to graves of Shamans that were buried by their tribes.

There is at least one group of cavemen or cave dwellers that are mentioned in the Bible. The Horim of Mt. Seir, in the region between the Dead Sea and the Gulf of Aqaba lived in dwellings carved out of sandstone. Many of their homes are found around the famous stone archaeological sites of Petra in Jordan. The Horim are associated with the ancient giants of Canaan along with the Anakim, Gibborim, Rephaim, and other tribes the Israelites came into contact with during their conquest of the Holy Land.

Cave dwellings and mountain shrines are important for Biblical archaeology because the cultures and tribes that would occupy the Fertile Crescent, Levant, and surrounding areas left behind vital clues to their ways of life. Semitic and non-Semitic cultures used mountains for gathering places for religious and cult purposes, places of refuge, and permanent dwelling places. Some Amorite tribes lived in mountains in Israel and Mesopotamia. Amorites are not a single people, but believed to be identified like the Hittites, who were identified with multiple groups of people aside from the Hittites in early Turkey, as being spread all over the Middle East as they were Semitic in origin similar to the Israelites.

The word used to identify many cult sites in Biblical

*Biblical Gilgal Location Courtesy of Rgrobman*

archaeology is *Gilgal*. Gilgal is identified in 1 Samuel 7:16 as the site King David was welcomed back from exile when his son Absalom attempted to usurp him as king. The definition of Gilgal is mentioned in the minor prophets books of Amos,

Hosea, and Micah. A Gilgal by Hebrew definition is a type of circle made of stones, and is a location of apostate worship. According to Joshua 5:2-11, a Gilgal or Gilgalim (plural) is where Israelite children where circumcised during the forty year wilderness wandering of the Israelites. Another Gilgal site was discovered at Mt. Gerizim.

Mt. Gerizim was where the Israelites renewed a covenant with God, and where the territories of the tribes of Israel were divided up. Mt. Gerizim is the site of a Passover feast that was referenced in Joshua 5:2-11, and conducted by the Israelites during their wanderings. The cultic significance of mountains to the Israelites plays an important function in what Adam Zertal referred to as a *Bamah*. The word bamah means a cultic site or high place. The identification of bamah as a high place further adds to certain mountains as holy.

High places are among the most powerful of symbols in religion, stories of heroes, and examples of places that miracles happened. Apart from the Israelite presence at Mt. Ebal and Mt. Gezirim are traces of other inhabitants of the region at the mountain sites. One unique find at the gilgal mountain sites was their shapes as shoes or sandals. Shoe symbols played a major part in Israelite and other non-Semitic peoples' ritual practices such as placing a foot on someone to signify a battle victory, or treading over a territory to show its subjugation to a master. The most mysterious foot symbols associated with gilgalim sites are found at the Ain Dara temple in northern Syria.

Large footprints are found carved into limestone floors of the Ain Dara temple. The footprints first appear in one limestone slab in a left and right pair. Another limestone slab above the first pair of feet is a single right foot imprint. Both limestone slabs measure out at three feet in length. Adam Zertal believes the feet represent symbols of Yahweh (God), the deity of the Israelite migrants to the area. However, it is possible the large 3 feet long footprints represent another group the Israelites would encounter during their conquest of Canaan. The group most likely associated with the Ain Dara temple footprints could be the giants that the Israelites encountered while conquering the Promised Land.

The giants of the Bible appear in several parts of the Bible. The Horim of Deuteronomy are one group or tribe of the giants that the Israelites referred to as related to the Nephilim. Twice the Horim are mentioned in the Bible in the book of Deuteronomy. Deuteronomy 2:12 KJV reads, *"The Horims also dwelt in Seir before time; but the children of Esau succeeded them, when they had destroyed them before them, and dwelt in their stead; as Israel did unto the land of his possession, which the Lord gave unto them."*

Deuteronomy 2:22 KJV states, *"As he did to the children of Esau, which dwelt in Seir, when he destroyed the Horims before them; and they succeeded them, and dwelt in their stead even unto this day."* The Horim were possibly related to the Zazzumim, Emim, and Rephaim of Canaan.

The Rephaim occupied the walled cities of Bashan. One of their kings is mentioned by name. The king of Bashan that is mentioned is named Og. Og is mentioned in the books of Psalms, Nehemiah, Deuteronomy, Joshua, Numbers, and 1 Kings. He is believed to be the last of the Rephaim, which is Hebrew for dreaded ones as well as defined as giant, and was also considered to be related to the Amorites. The mention of the brief details of the other tribes of the giants is to show similar characteristics of the Horim.

The Horim are likely inhabitants of Mt. Seir before even the arrival of Abraham in the land of Canaan. The mention in Deuteronomy 2:12 of the Horim dwelling in Seir "before time" could denote a Stone Age origin. After the arrival of the Edomites into the area of Seir, the Horim did mix and intermarry with the Edomites. The Horim are also identified as Horites in Genesis 14:6, where one of the tribes of giants is defeated by the army of Cherdorlaomer in what is called the "War of the Kings."

The Horim were aboriginal people when they dwelt in Mt. Seir. The word aboriginal is defined as anything (plant, human, or animal) that inhabited or existed in a land from earlier times before the arrival of later settlers. In a shorter definition, an aborigine is something indigenous (originating or naturally occurring) to an area. It is likely the Horim culture, in conjunction with the Deuteronomy 2:12 *before time* reference, is a far older civilization. However, such a statement is still only a theory due to the lack of archeological and carbon dating evidence.

The wording that is used throughout the Bible needs to be carefully studied in order to reveal the mysteries that go unnoticed by common readers. While not exactly known, the Bible does seem to point to a timeline far older than most people realize. I have always believed that the Bible spans a timeline of 10,000 years and possibly older. With the research of such words as *before time* and other defining phrases spread throughout scripture adds further evidence to my theories to help prove them on many levels.

# FIELD NOTES

The pursuit of knowledge through archaeology is one of the greatest sciences available to mankind. The adapting of the science of archaeology to the lands and people of the Bible make the Word of God come alive in brand new ways. The unlocking of the mysteries of the Bible help to allow the undertaking of going deeper in the revelations which prove the existence of everything that occurred in the Bible's history.

God developed mankind to adapt and grow with change. He made all life that way. One scripture favored with that idea is Romans 1:20 KJV *"For the invisible things of Him from the creation of the world are clearly seen, being understood by the things that are made, even His eternal power and Godhead; so that they are without excuse."* People can see God's hand in everything that walks and talks on the face of the earth. God's creations adapt and grow to be better just like He had planned from the very beginning. Biblical archaeology is one science that can show such growth.

God designed all His creations to adapt to change. Evidence of this is seen throughout the Bible. In science books and magazines people read about life adapting to meet the changing times and environments. Environments (with an *s* for plural) are used because each part of the world produces several different environmental conditions unique to the different areas of the earth. Weather patterns, climate changes, temperatures, and all other areas of nature are different throughout the world. As mentioned, the Bible can use the study of ecology to see how the Holy Land and surrounding areas were affected by the environmental factors of the Bible. Such an application would only strengthen the evidence to show the truth behind the history of the Bible.

Those different environmental factors can make all things living adapt and change to current and future environmental differences in order to survive and thrive. People of the Bible are among some of the most "adapt to change" individuals and groups in existence. Some people in the Bible survived into the modern world, while others became extinct. If people take into account the fact that the earth is dated to be millions to billions of years old, then it would only be natural to assume all life was designed to grow with changes or to die out like dinosaurs and other species. Possibly, the Bible covers a timeline of over 10,000 years rather than the estimated 6,000 years time span many believe it covers historically. The study of the Natufian and Ubaidian cultures help to prove the span of tens of thousands of years of existence, which adds further intrigue to studying Biblical timelines and gives validity to the theory of a great time lapse between Genesis 1:1 and Genesis 1:2.

Moses, the author of the first five books of the Bible called the Torah (and some scholars believe was also the author of the book of Job) lived in a time when many histories and sciences were in existence throughout the early empires. Moses had access to these histories and sciences by way of his adoption as a member of the Egyptian royal family. It is plausible to say he was educated on civilizations, timelines, and the sciences of the day that only the most enlightened minds (scholars and tutors) would share with him due to his status as a prince of Egypt. Aside from Moses are other accounts spread throughout the Bible by the various authors.

To explore each and every piece of archaeological evidence both in the literal and physical realm of the Bible is the reason to undertake Biblical archaeology. The most important purpose however is to unlock the even deeper parts of the Bible. What if a giant of Tsz-Nephilimus Sapiens could be discovered in some cave site near Petra? What if a hidden gilgal was discovered somewhere in an unknown part of the Middle East that had traces of Semitic or proto Semitic connections? What would the odds be that a piece of evidence to prove once and for all the existence of Jewish ties to the Holy Land could be found in some unmarked location simply by chance? Those are the questions that surround Biblical archaeology, yet is the reason that the science exists. If new discoveries can continue to be made, then more facts surrounding the Bible and the history that God was involved in can be shown more and more each day. Such a pursuit is putting faith into action. Faith that is action is faith that works. Faith without works is dead (James 2:17).

# BIBLIOGRAPHY & SOURCES FOR PHOTOS

Abegg Jr., Martin, and Cook, Edward, Wise, Michael, *The Dead Sea Scrolls.* New York, NY: Harper Collins Publishing, 2005.

Al-Tihami, Muhammad Hasan Muhammad. *"Suyuf al-Rasul wa 'uddahharbi-hi.'* Cairo: Hijr, 1992.
http://www.usna.edu/users/humss/bwheller/swords/batar.html

Bacher, Wilhelm; Prince, John Dyneley; M. Seligsohn. "Teraphim."*JewishEncyclopedia.*1906.www.jewishencyclopedia.com/articles/14331-teraphim.

Bahn, Paul, Ed. *The Complete Illustrated History of World Archaeology.* Blaby Road, Wingston Leicestershire: Lorenz Books, 2013.

Bird-David, Nurit. "Animism" Revisited: Personhood, Environment, and Relational

Epistemology." *Current Anthropology.* 40 (S1): S67. Doi: 10.1086/200061. 1999.

https://en.wikipedia.org/wiki/Animism.

Capwell, Tobias, and Withers, Harvey J.S., *The Complete Illustrated History of Knives, Swords, Spears, & Daggers.* China: Annes Publishing Ltd., 2013.

Carter, Robert A., Philip, Graham. *Deconstructing the Ubaid.* Carter, Robert A., Philip, Graham (eds). *Beyond the Ubaid: Transformation and Integration in the Late Prehistoric Societies of the Middle East.* Chicago: The Oriental Institute of the University ofChicago.P.2.2010.http://i.uchicago.edu/sites/oi.uchicago.edu/files/uploads/shared/docs/saoc63.pdf.

Carter, Robert. "The Neolithic Origins of Seafaring in the ArabianGulf."*Aijournal.com*.2002.www.aijournal.com/articles/abstract/10.5334/ai.0613/.

Coleman, J.A., *The Dictionary of Mythology*. China: Arcturus, 2015.

*Collins Dictionary of Science.* Glasgow, Scotland: HarperCollins Publishers, 2003.

Cutler, Catherine, Russell, Tony, and Walters, Martin, *Trees of The World.* London, England: Hermes House, 2007.

Day, Michael. "Fossil Reanalysis Pushes Back Origin of HomoSapiens."*NatureAmerica,Inc.*2017.
http://www.scientificamerican.com/article/fossil-reanalysis-pushes/.

Doody,David. *"WhyHunt."Utne.com*.2011.www.utne.com/mind-and-body/why-hunt-hunting-human-core.

E. Strouhal. "Five Plastered Skulls from Pre-Pottery Neolithic B Jericho: Anthropological Study." *Paleorient.* P. 231-247. 1973.www.persee.fr/doc/paleo_0153_9345_1973_num_1_2_4169.

Files, John. "Three-Age System." *Encompass88.blogspot.com*. 2015.encompass88.blogspot.com/2015/09/Mesopotamia-prerequisite.html?m+1.

Flaherty, Thomas H. ed., "The Pioneers of Civilization." *Sumer: Cities of Eden.* 158-159. Richmond, Virginia: Time Life Books, 1993.

Garrod, D.A.E. Excavation of a Paleolithic Cave In Western Judea, Quarterly Statement of the Palestine Exploration Fund 60:1825.1928.www.tandfonline.com/doi/abs/10.1179/peq.1928.60.4.182?journalCode=ypeq20.

Glossary of Landform and Geologic Terms. *National Soil Survey Handbook Part 629*. National Cooperative Soil Survey. Nrcs.usda.gov.2010.https://www.nrcs.usda.gov/Internet?FS E_DOCUMENTS/nrcs142p2_052234.doc.

Gordon, Cyrus H., *The Ancient Near East.* New York, NY: Ventor Publishers, Inc., 1965.

Griggs, Mary Beth, "Egypt's Forgotten Dynasty*" Archaeology.* July/August. (2014). 49-52.

Harris, M.H., ed., *Hebraic Literature Translations From The Talmud, Midrashim, And Kabbala.* New York, NY: Tudor Publishing Co., 1936.

Harris, Stephen L., *"Understanding the Bible."* Palo alto: Mayfield.1985.https://en.m.wikipedia.org/wiki/Nimrod.

Hawkins, Ralph K., "Israelite Footprints*" Biblical Archaeology Review.* March/April Vol. 42. 2016.

Hutchins, Robert Maynard, Ed., *Herodotus Thucydides.* Chicago, IL: EncyclopediaBritannica, Inc., 1952.

IAC Publishing, LLC. "What Was The Population of Mesopotamia?*"www.reference.com.*2017.http://www.reference.c om/history/population-mesopotamia-9e7a0f4732b9b.

Kempinski, Aharon. "The Hittites Between tradition and History," *Biblical Archaeology Review*, Vol. 42, No. 2. March/April (2016).

Kiel, Yishai. "Abraham and Nimrod in the Shadow of Zarathustra.*"TheJournalofReligion.*2015.www.journals.uchicago. edu/doi/pdf/10.1086/678533.

Leakey, Richard, and Lewin, Roger, *Origins Reconsidered.* New

York NY: AnchorBooks, 1992.

Lewis,BernardE."WhoAretheSemites?"*myjewishlearning.com*.200
3.www.myjewishlearning.com/article/who-are-the-semites/.

Lovgren, Stefan. "Is Troy True? The Evidence Behind Movie
Myth."*News.nationalgeographic.com*.2004.News.nationalgeographi
c.com/news/2004/05/0514_040514_troy.html.

Luhr, James F., ed., *Earth*.  New York, NY: DK Publishing,
Inc., 2009.

Mazar, Amihai, *Archaeology of The Land of The Bible- 10,000-586
B.C.E.* New York, NY: Doubleday, 1992.

Marzulli, L.A, *On The Trail of The Nephilim*. Los Angeles, CA:
Spiral of Life Publishing, 2013.

Nalbandian, Garegin D., *The Legend of Hayk and Bel Nimrod*.
Baltimore, MA: Publish America, 2013.

New International Version, *Life Application Study Bible*. Grand
Rapids, MI: Zondervan, 2011.

Oral Roberts Edition. *Holy Bible King James Version*. Tulsa,
OK: Oral Roberts Evangelistic Association, Inc., 1981.

Peled, Ilan, and White, Ellen, 'The Hittites Between
Tradition and History" *Biblical Archaeology Review*. March/April
Vol. 42, (2016). 38.

Por, F.D. "The Levantine: and bridge: Historical and Present
Patterns."*Nativefishlab.net*.2017.www.nativefishlab.net/library/
textpdf/18634.pdf.

Quayle, Stephen, *Genesis 6 Giants*.  Bozeman, MT: End Times
Publishers, 2013.

Ralph K. Hawkins, "The Iron Age I Structure on Mt. Ebal: Excavation and Interpretation." *Biblical Archaeology Review.* Winona Lake, IN: Eisenbrauns, (2012). 219.

Ralphs.Solecki, Rose L. Solecki, and Anagnostis P. Agelarakis. "The Proto-Neolithic Cemetery in Shanidar Cave." *Tamupress.com.* Texas A&M University Press. PP. 3-5 ISBN 978158442720.2004.www.tamupress.com/product/Proto-Neoplithic-Cemetary-in-Shanidar Cave,78.aspx.

Rea, Cam, *March of The Scythians.* San Bernardino, CA: Rea Publishing, 2015.

Reuters. "Israel Furious After UNESCO Jerusalem Resolution."*Huffpost.com.*2016.m.huffpost.com/us/entry/us_5 800c139e4b0e8c198a76ec6.

Scarpari, Marurizio, *Ancient China.* New York, NY: Barnes & Nobles, Inc., 2000.

Steele, Katie and Stefansson, H. Orri, "Decision Theory" *The Stanford Encyclopedia of Philosophy* (Winter 2015 Edition), EdwardN.Zalta(ed.).2015.https://en.m.wikipedia.org/wiki/D ecision_theory.

*The English Standard Version Study Bible.* Wheaton, IL: Crossway, 2008.

*The Nelson Study Bible.* Nashville, TN: Thomas Nelson Publishers, 1997.

*The New Bible Dictionary;* ed. J. D. Douglas; InterVarsity Fellowship, 1962, @by W. B. Eerdmans Publishing Co.; p. 1253. Kukis.org/Doctrines/Teraphim.pdf.

Vitebsky, Piers. "Hunters, Herders, and Gatherers." *The Shaman*. London, England: Duncan Baird Publishers, 1995.

Wadley, L; Hodgskiss, T; Grant, M. "Implications for Complex Cognition from the Hafting of tools with Compound Adhesives in the Middle Stone Age. South Africa." *Proceedings of the National Academy of Sciences of the United StatesofAmerica*.106(24):95904....Bibcode:2009PNAS..106.959 0W. doi:10.1073/pnas.090057106. ISSN 0027-8424. PMC 200998.PMID19433786.2009.http://en.m.wikipedia.org/wiki /adhesive#/search.

Wells, H.G., *The Outline of History*. Garden City, NY: Garden City Books, 1961.

Zukeran, Patrick. "The World View of Animism." *Bible.org*. 2010. http://bible.org/article/world-animism.

## PHOTO SOURCES:

# ABOUT THE AUTHOR

Dr. Harry Assad Salem III is author of over ten books including children's literature and scholarly studies. He is a graduate of California State University San Bernardino, Newburgh Seminary and College of the Bible, and Heritage University and Seminary.

Dr. Salem holds five earned doctorates in archaeology, biblical studies, theology, religious education, and practical ministry. He also holds an honorary doctorate in divinity. Dr. Salem is the creator of the children's book series Learning Pals that he created to teach children about ethics and morals.

He has been an ordained minister with Salem Family Ministries for over ten years. Dr. Salem is also a world class strongman and champion powerlifter with several championships and titles. His motto is "Excellence is excellent," and makes the effort to live every day by a standard of excellence for success and prosperity.

## Books by Dr. Harry Assad Salem III

Grave Raiders

Sound of The Spirit

Feminine Spirits & Angels

Age of Mystery Series:

Age of Mystery

Grave Raiders

Learning Pals Children's Series:

Count of Ten Say Amen *Children's Book*

Ten Steps to Build and be Spirit Filled *Children's Book*

Counting Ten Fingers for Patience *Children's Book*

Ten Shots for Do and Don't *Children's Book*

I would love to hear from you. There are many ways to stay connected to me. You can contact me either through the mail or the internet at the ministry website.

**Salem Family Ministries**
**P.O. Box 1595**
**Cathedral City, CA 92235**
**www.salemfamilyministries.org**

.

www.ingramcontent.com/pod-product-compliance
Lightning Source LLC
Chambersburg PA
CBHW072349090426
42741CB00012B/2983